To

Bless

Making It Count

A Life Well Lived

Written by: Tim Gregory, Ph.D.

Table of Contents

Introduction

"Look, the highest heavens and the earth and everything in it all belong to the Lord your God." Deuteronomy 10:14 (NLT)

It was a regular afternoon, nothing special that I can recall, when my phone rang. On the other end of the line was an old missionary, Don Normand. Don and his wife had served the Lord for many years in South Africa. Now, well into their senior years, Don and his wife were living in Florida, where he continued to share the wisdom and experiences he had gained through his many years of serving the Lord with other ministers. Don's health was poor at this point in his life, and his medical bills had far surpassed his income. Don had called with a request. He wanted to know if the church I pastored could help him with his medical expenses. Don had been a friend of the church, ministering there on several occasions in the past. I told Don we'd be happy to help him with his medical expenses.

As I inquired of the Lord how much money we should send Don, the Lord gave me a specific amount that exceeded what I had originally considered, but I made a choice to listen to God and send the amount of money He had told us to send. The check was written the next day, and I took it to the post office to mail off. After dropping the check in the mail, I stopped by to check the church's post-office-box. In the mail was a letter, and check, from a couple who had visited our church once (maybe twice) and had now sold their home. They wanted to give an offering to the church from the proceeds they had received from the sale of their home. The check they had written was for more than double what the Lord had instructed us to give to Don! God had provided for us before we had ever said "*yes*" to Don's request. Of course, God knew what we would do, and that we would be obedient to His leading, and as such, had prepared beforehand that we would be more than supplied with the funds needed to help Don, and he even multiplied a financial blessing back to the church, so that we may continue to advance the Kingdom and be a blessing to others.

This is only one example of the many ways I have experienced God's blessing in my ministry and personal life. I have learned throughout the years that the blessings of the Kingdom are for the children of the King! This is so they may be abundantly supplied to do the work their Father and King has called them to. It is my desire in writing this book to pass on this truth to my brothers and sisters in Christ.

I understand, without reserve, that all of God's blessings are not financial in nature. There can be no doubt of this truth. Yet, throughout my travels abroad and my ministry at home, I have consistently seen God's children hindered by a lack of financial provision; basing what they can and cannot do on the amount of money they have, or, the lack thereof. I have witnessed this lack of financial provision hindering their life and ministry in this world, creating both frustration and disappointment. While all the time, their Father possesses the abundance of this world, and He has in no way called them to be beggars of bread or money. But, has provided for them to live and serve Him in His abundance.

As the children of Israel readied themselves to enter the land God had promised to Abraham, the Lord told them:

> If you fully obey the Lord your God and carefully keep all his commands that I am giving you today, the Lord

your God will set you high above all the nations of the world. You will experience all these blessings if you obey the Lord your God: Your towns and your fields will be blessed. Your children and your crops will be blessed. The offspring of your herds and flocks will be blessed. Your fruit baskets and breadboards will be blessed. Wherever you go and whatever you do, you will be blessed. The Lord will conquer your enemies when they attack you. They will attack you from one direction, but they will scatter from you in seven! The Lord will guarantee a blessing on everything you do and will fill your storehouses with grain. The Lord your God will bless you in the land he is giving you. If you obey the commands of the Lord your God and walk in his ways, the Lord will establish you as his holy people as he swore he would do. Then all the nations of the world will see that you are a people claimed by the Lord, and they will stand in awe of you (Deuteronomy 28:1-10, NLT).

God was simply telling them, that if they would only obey and follow His ways, they would be blessed in every way! In fact, they would be blessed to a point that would bring those who see them to stand in awe! This blessing was for Israel and was contingent upon their obedience to God's commands. Yet, as God's children today, we find His blessing rests upon us, not because of our works, but because of the work of Jesus Christ our Lord. This blessing includes the abundance of God's provision to all areas of our lives.

As we follow the commands of our Lord Jesus Christ, acting in faith, we will walk closely to our Heavenly Father, who is the giver of all good things. When we are close to our Heavenly Father, we are able to receive all Jesus has earned for us through

His obedience. But, when we allow fear and doubt to motivate us to walk in disobedience to the commands of Jesus, we miss the abounding blessings of God. Now, those blessings cannot be earned, and our Father is always ready to freely and abundantly give them to all His children. But, when we walk in obedience, out of a heart of love that overflows with faith, we draw close to our Heavenly Father, and when that happens, we are in a position to receive all God has for us, which includes financial blessings. When fear and doubt fill our hearts, we are moved to act in disobedience, which leads us away from our Father and puts us out of position to receive God's wonderful blessings. Obedience to Jesus is nothing more than an outward expression of an inward faith, and it is only by faith that we can receive anything from the Lord!

Thomas Watson was a very influential English, non-conformist, Puritan preacher and author of the 17th century. He once said, *"Water is useful to the ship and helps it to sail better to the haven, but let the water get into the ship, if it is not pumped out, it drowns the ship. So riches are useful and convenient for our passage. We sail more comfortably with them through the troubles of this world; but if the water gets into the ship, if love of riches gets into the heart, then we are drowned by them."*

The riches of this world are nothing more than a tool to complete the work Jesus has given us to do before we leave and go to our true home in Heaven. Since we currently reside in a physical world that uses a tangible currency, we'll find it useful and even needful in most cases to have an adequate supply of that currency, as we set out to advance the Kingdom of our Lord. There is no shame in having an adequate supply of finances at our disposal to advance the Kingdom of our God with, as long as it is used wisely, and never makes its way into our hearts.

Gregory of Nyssa lived and ministered in the fourth century. He served as the bishop of Nyssa from 372 until his death in 394. Gregory wrote a message entitled *On the Love of the Poor* in which he elaborated on the concepts of rich and poor, and the practical role that wealth was to play in the life of those who were committed to following Jesus. Gregory said:

> *Let us keep the supreme and first law of God, who sends rain on the just and the sinners, and makes the sun rise equally on all. He has spread out the unoccupied land for everyone on earth, with springs and rivers and forests; he has given air for the winged species, and water for all aquatic creatures; he generously provides the basic elements of life to all without subjecting them to any power of force, any limits of law, or any divisions of geographical boundaries. No, he has set forth all of the same necessities as the common possessions of all, so that no one would lack anything. In this way, he honors the equality of nature by the equality of the gifts, and displays the abundance of his goodness. But human beings, in contrast, bury gold and silver and soft, superfluous clothing in the ground, as well as their glittering jewels and other similar kind, which bear the signs of war and discord and the first act of rebellion; they then raise their eyebrows in perplexity and refuse to show mercy to the unfortunate who are their natural kin. They neither wish to help those in need out of their surplus—what perversity! what foolishness!—nor do they even consider this fact: that what we call poverty and wealth, freedom and slavery, and other, similar names,*

10

were introduced into human history at a later stage as a sort of epidemics that assault us accompanying sin, and is a symptom of it. But, as Scriptures says, "from the beginning it was not so." The One who created the human person in the beginning made him free and endowed him with free will, subject only to the law of his commandment, and rich in the delights of Paradise. And God desired to bestow the same freedom on the rest of the human race, through the single seed of the first common ancestor. Freedom and wealth consisted simply in keeping the commandment, whereas true poverty and slavery came from its transgression.

The blessings of the Kingdom are truly for the children of the King, so that they may be able to purposely and aggressively advance the Kingdom of their God! It has been said, *"Give a man a fish and he'll eat for a day, but teach him to fish and he'll eat for a lifetime."* My prayer is that this book will serve as a tool to help my brothers and sisters in Christ to live free of financial frustrations, not dependent or looking to man for financial help, but completely and totally dependent on their God, embracing the command of their Lord to take the Gospel throughout the world and to make disciples of all mankind, helping the helpless, destroying all the works of the devil, and glorifying their God in all they do! And as such, blessed abundantly in every way as they go forward advancing the Kingdom of Jesus Christ their Lord!

Chapter 1

Humility Receives the Blessing

"Now there were some present at that time who told Jesus about the Galileans whose blood Pilate had mixed with their sacrifices." Luke 13:1 (NIV)

It was brought to the attention of Jesus two particular incidents, which ended in tragedy. The first was a political affair in-which Pilate had several Galileans killed, and allowed their blood to be mixed with that of the Temple sacrifice. The second incident was that of a natural disaster in-which something caused a tower in Siloam to fall, killing eighteen people. In ancient times when bad things happened it was a normal reaction of people to assume that the sins of a person brought the destruction they had experienced upon them. They were getting what they deserved, or perhaps, reaping what they had sown. It was supposed that good and evil came upon an individual based off of their behavior.

It's easy to see how this attitude could cause one's pride to rise up; to look up on others and suppose you were better than those who had experienced tragedy. Jesus clarifies the matter when He says, *"Do you think that these Galileans were worse sinners than all the other Galileans because they suffered this way? I tell you, no! But unless you repent, you too will all perish"* (Luke 13:2, NIV). Any thought of superiority that the people might have felt over those who lost their lives in these two events, Jesus quickly and directly put to rest.

The idea here is that those who are spared the heartache of going through such a loss should be humble and grateful, for they are no more deserving of God's grace than someone else. Grace is free and cannot be earned! Therefore, we have no room to feel that we have accomplished some form of righteous achievement because we experienced the grace of God and someone else did not. Yet, pride is sneaky, and takes every opportunity it can find to rise up in the child of God and lead them into destruction and away from the grace of God. This is why the Scriptures say, *"Pride goes before destruction, and a haughty spirit before a fall"* (Proverbs 16:18, NRSV).

In 2005, Hurricane Katrina devastated the city of New Orleans. When this happened, many in the Church were quick to point out the riotous living that went on in the city, and that surely the destruction that Katrina brought was nothing more than the judgement of God falling on a corrupt and wicked people. It was an opportunity for pride to rise up in the hearts of men and women in the Church, which led them away from God's grace, and into a this-for-that mindset. This mindset, which is ignited by pride, causes us to miss God's grace every time!

The truth is, the people of New Orleans were no more deserving of judgement than anyone else, for all have fallen short of the glory of God and all are in need of His grace. The city of New Orleans is home to many of the followers of Christ, who suffered terribly from this hurricane. When tragedy strikes, and we are spared, our attitude should always be one of humility and gratefulness, for we have not earned God's mercy and grace, but have freely received it through no effort of our own. Always remember, *"For it is by grace you have been saved, through faith —and this is not from yourselves, it is the gift of God— not by works, so that no one can boast"* (Ephesians 2:8-9, NIV). Both boasting and pointing of the finger are expressions of pride, and both will cause us to miss the grace of God.

Justified

Jesus relays a story of a tax collector and a Pharisee who went up to the Temple to pray, in response to those who were confident of their own righteousness and looked down on others. The tax collectors of the time were well-known for cheating and stealing; they were despised by most people. The Pharisee was to be a picture of right living, in accordance to God's Word. When they went up to the Temple the two men prayed, revealing the content of their heart. *"The Pharisee stood by himself and prayed: 'God, I thank you that I am not like other people—robbers, evildoers, adulterers—or even like this tax collector. I fast twice a week and give a tenth of all I get.' But the tax collector stood at a distance. He would not even look up to heaven, but beat his breast and said, 'God, have mercy on me, a sinner'"* (Luke 18:11-13, NIV).

The Pharisee was proud that he had done all the right things, he was confident that those works were sure to justify him before God. The Pharisee was certain that he was deserving of God's grace, because of the good things he had done. The tax collector in no way attempted to justify himself before God. He didn't speak of his position or any of his works, he simply humbled himself in hopes of receiving God's grace. It is in his humility that the tax collector finds the grace of God! On the other hand, it is in his pride that the Pharisee misses the grace of God. In speaking of the tax collector, Jesus says, *"I tell you that this man, rather than the other, went home justified before God. For all those who exalt themselves will be humbled, and those who humble themselves will be exalted"* (Luke 18:14, NIV).

If you want to live in the abundant blessings that come from the grace of God, apart from your works, stay humble! Never lift your works or deeds up before God, for this will only invite pride into your heart, which will surely reap untold havoc in your life, causing disappointment and confusion. God's grace is freely given and must be freely received! *"But now God has shown us a way to be made right with him without keeping the requirements of the law, as was promised in the writings of Moses and the prophets long ago. We are made right with God by placing our faith in Jesus Christ. And this is true for everyone who believes, no matter who we are. For everyone has sinned; we all fall short of God's glorious standard. Yet God, in his grace, freely makes us right in his sight. He did this through Christ Jesus when he freed us from the penalty for our sins"* (Romans 3:21-24, NLT).

Humility opens wide the door, through which God's grace freely flows, but pride slams the door shut! Stay humble and you will stay blessed!

The Power of Humility

"For the Lord takes delight in his people; He crowns the humble with victory." Psalm 149:4 (NIV)

The crown of victory belongs to God, and He freely gives it to the humble! The victory, the blessings, and everything that is good, which men try to win by their accomplishments and deeds, God freely crowns the humble with. Humility ushers in the blessings of God! Humility is a powerful catalyst that causes the blessings of our Heavenly Father to overtake us! Where humility is absent, so will be the blessings of God. Humility achieves what the works and deeds of men and women could never do!

Humility of a Soldier

The Bible tells of King Ahaziah of Israel, and of a time when he was gravely injured. The king sends a messenger to the temple of Baal-zebub, the god of Ekron, to ask whether he would recover. The messenger is met by the Prophet Elijah, with a message for the king. Elijah tells the messenger that because the king did not seek out the God of Israel, but instead turned to a demonic god, that he would surely die.

When the messenger returns, and relays Elijah's message back to the king and the king becomes furious. He sends a captain of the army with fifty men to bring Elijah back to him. When the captain approaches Elijah, he attempts to exercise the authority and power he feels he rightfully holds. The captain surely takes great pride in his position of power, but his man given authority and power will yield him no success while confronting God's prophet on earth. Fire comes down from heaven and consumes the captain and his men. In response, King Ahaziah sends another captain with another troop of fifty soldiers. Again, the captain attempts to exercise his authority and power over Elijah and again fire comes down from heaven and consumes him and his men.

A third captain and fifty more soldiers are sent out by the king, but this captain takes a very different approach then the first two did. This time *"the captain went up the hill and fell to his knees before Elijah. He pleaded with him, 'O man of God, please spare my life and the lives of these, your fifty servants. See how the fire from heaven came down and destroyed the first two groups. But now please spare my life'"* (2 Kings 1:13-14, NLT)!

His humility gets the attention of God, who responds in a positive way, telling Elijah, *"Go down with him, and don't be afraid of him"* (2 Kings 1:15, NLT).

A true attitude of humility brought the third captain success in his mission. The captain didn't rely on his positional power or the physical strength of the soldiers that were with him (as the captains before him had done), but instead, humbles himself before the servant of the Lord, and in-turn, is exalted by God. Humility opened the door for the blessings of God to flow through, where pride had slammed the door shut for the first two captains! *"The Lord supports the humble, but he brings the wicked down into the dust"* (Psalm 147:6, NLT). Do you want the Lord to

> "Do you wish to rise? Begin by descending. You plan a tower that will pierce the clouds? Lay first the foundation of humility."
>
> Augustine of Hippo

support and bless the things you put your hands too? If you do, then stay humble! Never exalt yourself before the Lord, but rather humble yourself, relying on His mercy and goodness, and He will lift you up and bring you success!

Humility Before the Blessing

God brought the children of Israel out of the bondage they were subjected to in Egypt and sought to bring them into the Land He had promised to their ancestors. This land would be one where the descendants of Jacob would experience the great blessings of God, but before they could receive this land, they would need to learn humility. When they were preparing to cross over into the Land of Promise, Moses tells them, *"Remember how the Lord your God led you through the wilderness for these forty years, humbling you and testing you to prove your character, and to find out whether or not you would obey his commands"* (Deuteronomy 8:2, NLT).

Humility would direct the children of Israel into the blessings of God, and an attitude of humility would be needed to sustain those blessings over them. Humility always precedes the blessings of God! Humility is like a magnet that draws the blessings of God towards us! Without humility it is impossible to freely receive God's grace, and it is only by the grace of God that we receive the blessings of God! Stay humble in all things, at all times, refusing to allow pride to fill your heart, and you will always be blessed by God!

Humility Brings Wisdom

"The fear of the Lord is the beginning of knowledge, but fools despise wisdom and instruction." Proverbs 1:7 (NIV)

Humility brings godly wisdom, for humility stands in awe of God! As followers of Christ we must understand that our God is the Creator of the entire Universe. He is truly our Father and our Friend, yet, He is much more than that. Our God is the King of kings and Lord of lords! Before the heavens and the earth were created, He existed, in fact, He is the One who brought them into existence! By the breath that passed through His lips, He spoke and brought everything into being!

True humility brings us to a place of reverent fear, as we consider who our God is and what He has done! Without a reverent fear of the Lord the followers of Christ will never walk in humility, and if they fail to walk in humility they will surely fail to experience the fullness of God's blessings. Fear of the Lord brings us to a place of understanding, where we see the Word of God as not a suggestion to be considered, but a command to be embraced and followed whole heartedly!

The Lord told the people of Jerusalem, *"Your wickedness will punish you; your backsliding will rebuke you. Consider then and realize how evil and bitter it is for you when you forsake the Lord your God and have no awe of me"* (Jeremiah 2:19, NIV). The people of Jerusalem still worshiped God in their religious ceremonies, but their hearts were removed from Him. They had lost the reverent fear that their ancestors once had. When we fail to stand in awe of God's majesty, we will never be able to live with an attitude of humility, and therefore, we will never have a spirit of wisdom.

Wisdom opens our eyes to innovative ideas and means by which the Lord may bless us. Without wisdom we lean on our own understanding, not allowing the Lord to direct our paths into the means by which He intends to bless us. Godly wisdom moves us to look to the Lord for direction, dismissing what the world declares as truth, and embracing every word of God, and the leading of His Spirit. We understand that there is a distinct difference between godly wisdom and earthly wisdom, the Scriptures tell us:

> If you are wise and understand God's ways, prove it by living an honorable life, doing good works with the humility that comes from wisdom. But if you are bitterly jealous and there is selfish ambition in your heart, don't cover up the truth with boasting and lying. For jealousy and selfishness are not God's kind of wisdom. Such things are earthly, unspiritual, and demonic. For

wherever there is jealousy and selfish ambition, there you will find disorder and evil of every kind (James 3:13-16, NLT).

With a humble spirit comes the ability to receive direction from the Lord, through both His spoken word and His written word. Hence, we become wise! But pride tells us we know best; rejecting God's word pride leans on its own understanding, believing it can figure things out on its own. Pride separates itself from God, becoming a fool, it misses the blessings of God. *"Pride leads to disgrace, but with humility comes wisdom"* (Proverbs 11:2, NLT).

The Bible teaches us that the *"Fear of the Lord teaches wisdom; humility precedes honor"* (Proverbs 15:33, NLT). The verse that immediately follows says, *"We can make our own plans, but the Lord gives the right answer"* (Proverbs 16:1, NLT). Make your own plans for your life to gain wealth, and you will be plagued with disappointment and failure. But, if you will yield to the Lord's guidance, submitting your ways to Him with a true attitude of humility, He'll direct you in the way you should go. You will walk in godly wisdom, a wisdom that cannot be found amongst the ways of men, and you will be blessed in every way, and your life will impact the Kingdom of your God for all eternity!

Humility of a King

"You save the humble but bring low those whose eyes are haughty" Psalm 18:27 (NIV)

Humility is truly a powerful instrument through which the grace of God moves! It brings the blessings of God to full realization in our lives in ways we could never manufacture ourselves.

Throughout the Bible we find many examples of humility opening the door for people to receive the blessings of God, and some of these people had failed miserably at following God's Law. Yet, their contrite spirit was not rejected by the Lord. We'll look at two distinctly different kings who experienced the blessings of God, by the grace of God, because of their humility and contrite spirit. These kings are Josiah, from the nation of Judah, and Ahab, from the nation of Israel.

Josiah

Josiah was only eight years old when he became king of Judah. Josiah's father and grandfather had both been evil leaders and had led the nation of Judah to worship pagan gods, and to practice abominations such as offering their children in the fire to these pagan gods. But Josiah was different than them both, he followed the Lord, doing what was right in the sight of God.

Those who had ruled before Josiah had neglected to maintain the Temple, and now it was in need of an overhaul. In the eighteenth year of his reign, Josiah orders that the Temple be repaired. While the Temple is being restored and cleaned the Book of the Law is found.

The book is taken before Josiah and read to him by Hilkiah the High Priest. The reading of this book had a profound effect on Josiah. He tears his clothes and sends representatives to the prophetess Huldah to enquire of the Lord. Josiah understands the evil his fathers have done, and how the people have neglected the commands of their God. He presumes that God's anger must be great, and, he is correct in his assumption! Huldah relays God's word to them saying, *"This is what the Lord says: I am going to bring disaster on this place and its people, according to everything written in the book the king of Judah has read. Because they have forsaken me and burned incense to other gods and aroused my anger by all the idols their hands have made, my anger will burn against this place and will not be quenched*" (2 Kings 22:16-17, NIV).

God's anger is clear and so is the judgment that is about to fall upon Jerusalem. But, the Lord has another word for King Josiah, He tells Josiah, "*Because your heart was responsive and you humbled yourself before the Lord when you heard what I have spoken against this place and its people—that they would become a curse and be laid waste —and because you tore your robes and wept in my presence, I also have heard you, declares the Lord. Therefore, I will gather you to your ancestors, and you will be buried in peace. Your eyes will not see all the disaster I am going to bring on this place*" (2 Kings 22:19-20, NIV).

Josiah's humility had opened the door for the grace of God to flow through. Josiah would be blessed with peace during his reign, and the destruction that was to come upon Jerusalem would not come to pass until after his death. Josiah was a godly king, and he followed after the ways of the Lord just as his ancestor David had. But it would not be his mere obedience to God's word that would bring the blessings of God to his life, but a heart that responded to the word of God in humility. Humility made the way for Josiah to freely receive the grace of God; apart from any of his works, Josiah was radically blessed by God!

Ahab

Ahab was a king of Israel, and, unlike Josiah, he did not follow God. In fact, the Bible says, "*Ahab son of Omri did more evil in the eyes of the Lord than any of those before him*" (1 Kings 16:30, NIV). Ahab and his wife Jezebel led the people of Israel to worship Baal and did more to make God angry than any of the kings before him. He and his wife waged war against the prophets of God, seeking them out and killing them.

One day, Ahab comes across a vineyard he desires to have. The owner, a man named Naboth, refuses to sell it to him. Ahab has great possessions, but in his greed, he's not satisfied, and sulks when Naboth refuses to sell him his land. Jezebel notices her husband is upset and devises an evil plot to take the land from Naboth. She finds some evil men to go along with her plan; these men make a false accusation about Naboth. Because of these accusations Naboth is stoned to death; leaving his vineyard open for Ahab to seize.

God is greatly angered by this wickedness and sends the Prophet Elijah to pronounce judgement on Ahab. The Bible record this, saying:

> Ahab said to Elijah, "So you have found me, my enemy!" "I have found you," he answered, "because you have sold yourself to do evil in the eyes of the Lord. He says, 'I am going to bring disaster on you. I will wipe out your descendants and cut off from Ahab every last male in Israel—slave or free. I will make your house like that of Jeroboam son of Nebat and that of Baasha son of Ahijah, because you have aroused my anger and have caused Israel to sin.' "And also concerning Jezebel the Lord says: 'Dogs will devour Jezebel by the wall of Jezreel.' "Dogs will eat those belonging to Ahab who

die in the city, and the birds will feed on those who die in the country." (1 Kings 21:20-24, NIV)

At this word the evil king is greatly distressed, he tears his clothes, puts on sackcloth, and fasts; he lays down in sackcloth and goes around meekly. All of these things are outward signs of an inwards humility and mourning. It would be this true humility that would get the attention of God and open the door for this evil king to receive the grace of God. The Bibles says, *"Then the word of the Lord came to Elijah the Tishbite: 'Have you noticed how Ahab has humbled himself before me? Because he has humbled himself, I will not bring this disaster in his day, but I will bring it on his house in the days of his son'"* (1 Kings 21:28-29, NIV).

Now, keep in mind what the Scriptures say about Ahab! *"There was never anyone like Ahab, who sold himself to do evil in the eyes of the Lord, urged on by Jezebel his wife. He behaved in the vilest manner by going after idols, like the Amorites the Lord drove out before Israel"* (1 Kings 21:25-26, NIV). Ahab was nothing like Josiah who feared the Lord and followed His commands. Ahab and his wife were evil to the core! Yet, even this evil king is able to receive the goodness of God through humility! Humility opened the door for Ahab to be radically blessed; freely receiving the grace of God!

Such is the power of humility to open the door to all the blessings of God! Humility obtains the blessings of God freely by grace, apart from anything it does! Stay humble and you will surely stay blessed, as the door of God's grace opens widely, and His blessings are abundantly manifested in your life!

False Humility

24

"Do not let anyone who delights in false humility and the worship of angels disqualify you. Such a person also goes into great detail about what they have seen; they are puffed up with idle notions by their unspiritual mind." Colossians 2:18 (NIV)

False humility has many of the outward signs that true humility does, but it lacks the conviction of heart and a contrite spirit, which true humility always carries. False humility is consumed with religious practices and public opinion. Like many of the Pharisees of Jesus' day, it seeks to gain honor in the eyes of men. Jesus said, *"When you fast, do not look somber as the hypocrites do, for they disfigure their faces to show others they are fasting. Truly I tell you, they have received their reward in full. But when you fast, put oil on your head and wash your face, so that it will not be obvious to others that you are fasting, but only to your Father, who is unseen; and your Father, who sees what is done in secret, will reward you"* (Matthew 6:16-18, NIV).

The hypocrites had only a false humility, for they were concerned with what men thought, they had no desire to please God. True humility is consumed with pleasing God, it is focused on God and His ways, it has no time, nor desire, to entertain people or to win their applause! True humility is clothed with sackcloth on the inside long before it shows up on the outside.

False humility can be easy to embrace for it looks so much like the real thing, but it has no power to open the door of God's grace. False humility is concerned with its works and feels justified by what it does. Rather than fully trusting in the works of Jesus, it mingles the works of Jesus with its own deeds. It is very much like a cake that has only been cooked on one side.

25

False humility ushers in disappointment and confusion. True humility is always a matter of the heart!

The Prophet Isaiah wrote, *"You humble yourselves by going through the motions of penance, bowing your heads like reeds bending in the wind. You dress in burlap and cover yourselves with ashes. Is this what you call fasting? Do you really think this will please the Lord"* (Isaiah 58:5, NLT)? False humility merely goes through the motions; it may fast, it may pray, it may bow down on its knees, but inside it is still consumed with its own works to win the favor of God. False humility embraces inner pride for what it has accomplished, filling the heart it closes the door of God's grace and misses the blessings of God.

All of God's children must be aware of false humility and hidden-inner pride. To guard ourselves from both of these, which feed off of each other and hinder us from receiving the fullness of our Lord's goodness, we would be wise to keep our hearts and minds clothed in humility!

Clothed in Humility

"In the same way, you who are younger must accept the authority of the elders. And all of you must clothe yourselves with humility in your dealings with one another, for 'God opposes the proud, but gives grace to the humble.' Humble yourselves therefore under the mighty hand of God, so that he may exalt you in due time." 1 Peter 5:5-6 (NRSV)

What does it mean to clothe yourself in humility? To be clothed with something, as the apostle uses it here, is a Greek manner of speech, which identifies a person as actually being that thing. Peter is literally telling the followers of Christ that they are to be humble, and this inner humility should be displayed in their outward behavior towards one another. The Greek word used here for *clothe* carries the meaning of an outward garment that would cover a person's clothing. This could be applied in two distinctively different ways in the culture of the time.

First, clothe could be used to signify an ornamental garment. This garment would have been used to display decorative ornaments made of silk twist, or perhaps colorful knots. It would have been used to gain the attention of others, and to bring attention to the one who wore it. It would be the equivalent of carrying around a trophy, or buying a new suite of clothing, so that others would take note of you and your achievements.

Second, clothe could be used to signify the apron worn by a servant or slave. This would not have been a decorative piece of clothing, but one used to protect the other garments of clothing that the servant or slave was wearing. It was an instrument of clothing that allowed the individual to properly do the work they were assigned.[1]

The Apostle Peter provides us with two distinctive attitudes, which carry two distinctive outcomes. The followers of Christ can choose to display their works and achievements, so that others may take note, and the praise of those who take note can be won. This individual is sure to find the door to God's grace closed tight! On the other hand, the follower of Christ can put on the apron of a servant, with the mind-set of their Master who did the same thing and put their hand to the work of the Kingdom; humbly submitted to their Master and His word. When this happens, the follower of Christ will find the Lord

---

[1] Clark, Adam (1831). Clark's Commentary

exalting them, as the door of His grace opens wide, and the blessings of God freely and abundantly flow into their lives.

Let us learn from Jesus:

> Who, being in very nature God, did not consider equality with God something to be used to his own advantage; rather, he made himself nothing by taking the very nature of a servant, being made in human likeness. And being found in appearance as a man, he humbled himself by becoming obedient to death — even death on a cross! Therefore, God exalted him to the highest place and gave him the name that is above every name (Philippians 2:6-9, NIV).

The Scriptures make it clear that the follower of Christ must continually maintain an attitude of humility if they are going to serve their Master. Without the apron of humility, they will never be able to properly complete the work their Master has assigned to them, for the prideful heart of their old nature will always take the lead (leading to destruction). They will live at the mercy of this world and the devil, and neither of which are known for showing mercy to the followers of Christ. Humility must be put on, so that it covers the pride of our old nature and protects our hearts and minds from the distractions of this sinful world and the attacks of our enemy.

In humility we draw close to God, and the closer we are to the Lord the more we will be blessed, and, the greater will be our works for His Kingdom. It is in our humility that we find God lifting us up and blessing us, but, in our pride, we will find the hand of God against us, as our lives are plagued with frustration and disappointment. Only when we stay clothed with humility can our lives exalt our Savior, and, only when we live to exalt Jesus will we experience the fullness of God's grace! James sheds more light on this when he writes:

> And he gives grace generously. As the Scriptures say, "God opposes the proud but gives grace to the humble." So humble yourselves before God. Resist the devil, and he will flee from you. Come close to God, and God will come close to you. Wash your hands, you sinners; purify your hearts, for your loyalty is divided between God and the world. Let there be tears for what you have done. Let there be sorrow and deep grief. Let there be sadness instead of laughter, and gloom instead of joy. Humble yourselves before the Lord, and he will lift you up in honor (James 4:6-10, NLT).

Only clothed in humility can we humble ourselves before God. And, only when we are humble before God can we effectively resist the devil. As servants of Christ we will never submit to our Master if we are not clothed in humility, and if we are not submitted to Him, we will certainly be submitted to the devil. Humility is a garment that protects us, and prepares us, to do the work of the Great Commission our Master has called us to do! Wearing the apron of humility also positions the servant of Christ to be exalted and blessed by their Master!

Picture the Humble Servant

In the Book of Exodus, God calls Moses to the great purpose He has for his life. Moses would lead the children of Israel out of Egypt by the power of God. Moses performs some of the greatest wonders in the Bible. How easy it would have been for this power to consume him, as it would have most people. But

Moses clothed himself with humility, and that humility guarded him against the temptations that most would have succumbed to in the position of power God had given him.

The Scriptures tell of a particular time when Aaron and Miriam rise up to accuse Moses. *"While they were at Hazeroth, Miriam and Aaron criticized Moses because he had married a Cushite woman. They said, 'Has the Lord spoken only through Moses? Hasn't he spoken through us, too?' But the Lord heard them. (Now Moses was very humble—more humble than any other person on earth.)"* (Numbers 12:1-3, NLT). Moses was both the most powerful person on earth and the most humble! This correlation should not be overlooked!

Moses could have easily taken matters with Aaron and Miriam into his own hands. Who were they to speak out against this powerful man of God, who was chosen by God Himself to lead the children of Israel? This could have been his attitude, but it wasn't. Humility protected him from the temptation of acting in pride, and Moses allowed God to take care of the situation. In humility, Moses cast his cares on God, and God took care of them for him.

Moses wasn't always a humble man. In fact, before he flees to the wilderness, we see a picture of an Egyptian prince trying to exalt himself before the children of Israel. The Scriptures paint this picture for us, when they speak about him growing up in Egypt, saying:

> Many years later, when Moses had grown up, he went out to visit his own people, the Hebrews, and he saw how hard they were forced to work. During his visit, he saw an Egyptian beating one of his fellow Hebrews. After

looking in all directions to make sure no one was watching, Moses killed the Egyptian and hid the body in the sand. The next day, when Moses went out to visit his people again, he saw two Hebrew men fighting. "Why are you beating up your friend?" Moses said to the one who had started the fight. The man replied, "Who appointed you to be our prince and judge? Are you going to kill me as you killed that Egyptian yesterday" (Exodus 2:11-14, NLT)?

The first century Jewish historian Josephus tells of Moses as being a great and powerful general over the Egyptian army. As a general over the armies of Egypt Moses would

"The higher a man is in grace. The lower he will be in his own esteem."

Charles Spurgeon

learn to depend on his own abilities and strengths; he was a leader who could get things done, a man of action. So, when he sees a Hebrew being abused, he takes matters into his own hands, as he is accustomed to doing, and kills the man. At this point in his life Moses is a man filled with pride; he is confident in his abilities as a mighty general.

Moses surely was chosen by God, but God would have to be the one to exalt him. He would not be able to lead the children of Israel by his own might; Moses would have to learn to trust God to fight for him, and to lead him into victory. It would take forty years for God to humble Moses and prepare him for the great purpose He had called him to. When Moses returned to Israel, he was a different man. Now, instead of being clothed in ornaments of pride, he wore an apron of humility…an apron of a servant who was submitted to his Master. This servant of God would move in the power and favor of God, because his garment was that of humility.

Humility opened the door for Moses to become the man God had called him to be, to move in great power, and to have the favor of God in all he did. If you want the blessings of God to overwhelm your life, if you want to accomplish the purpose for which God has redeemed you, and if you want the power and favor of God to be with you in all you do, stay clothed in humility. Remember, your inner humility will always be evident in your outward actions! Stay humble and you will stay abundantly blessed by God, as the favor of God causes your hands to prosper at whatever they do!

Application and Self-Reflection

1. How would you describe pride?

_____

_____

_____

2. How do you understand the relationship between your actions and the blessings God desires to give you?

_____

_____

_____

3. How has pride hindered you in the past?

_____

_____

_____

4. How can you avoid this in the future?

_____

_____

_____

5. Describe what humility looks like to you?

_____

_____

_____

6. How can you maintain an attitude of humility, not allowing pride to lead you away from the free grace of God?

_____

_____

_____

Chapter 2

Reasons for the Blessing

"Tell those rich in this world's wealth to quit being so full of themselves and so obsessed with money, which is here today and gone tomorrow. Tell them to go after God, who piles on all the riches we could ever manage—to do good, to be rich in helping others, to be extravagantly generous. If they do that, they'll build a treasury that will last, gaining life that is truly life." 1 Timothy 6:17-19 (MSG)

In the church I pastor, the work of the Great Commission takes center stage. This work, and the mentality that goes with it, permeates every part of the church, and as such we are committed to pouring our resources into spreading the Gospel message and making disciples. Each year we distribute a significant percentage of our income to world missions, and that amount has steadily increased throughout the years I have pastored at Family Worship Center.

Back around 2014, during our annual mission conference, I was asked how much of our income we had given to the cause of world missions. This was a significant question, because unlike similar church organizations we don't run by a predetermined budget. Years ago, God spoke to me and moved me to do away with our pre-planned budgeting. The Lord assured me that He would continually provide for all we did, if I would simply trust Him and put the mission of the Great Commission first in all I led the church to do. And, He has definitely lived up to His part of the bargain!

As God continues to provide, we simply apply the finances we are blessed with to the work of the Great Commission around the world and at home in our local city and county. So, when I was asked this question I had to pause, I had no budgeted amount that had been predetermined that I could tell her, and I suddenly realized that I hadn't even looked at the end of the year financial reports yet. That year had finished the same way it started; with a bang! We were so busy with all the things God was allowing us to do, that we hadn't slowed down to look where all the finances were going. After the conferences that evening I took time to look at the financial records, which the accounting firm that keeps our books had prepared. I was shocked to see that we had used over 50% of every dollar that came in on world missions! I knew we had put a lot of our financial resources to the work of missions, but I didn't realize how much. We were simply using the money God provided us with for the Mission He had given us. God had abundantly blessed us financially and allowed us to use those finances to bring glory to His name, both around the world and in our own hometown.

I say this in no way to brag or boast, for I realize it is only by the grace of God we were able to do such a thing. I recently heard from a fellow minister friend of mine, that a church he is associated with gave 80% of their finances to the work of the Great Commission in one year. That's incredible!!

I tell this story to make a point. There is a reason individual believers and churches need the financial blessings of God. It's for the work of the Great Commission, and not for their own selfish desires. James addresses this same issue, as he speaks about receiving through prayer, when he says, *"Yet you don't have what you want because you don't ask God for it. And even when you ask, you don't get it because your motives are all wrong—you want only what will give you pleasure"* (James 4:2-3, NLT). Many of God's children face the same problem when it comes to money, they only want to satisfy their own desires. I believe it is for this reason that the idea of Christians having wealth has gained such a negative image.

Remember, the blessing of the Kingdom is indeed for the children of the King, but the children of the King are to use that blessing for the work of the Kingdom! When this happens, money has no chance of making it into the hearts of God's children, and they use it just as they would a hammer or any other tool, to build the Kingdom of their Lord. At this point, money is a good thing, and profits both the individual believer and the Kingdom!

The Church of Jesus Christ, made up of believers from around the world attending different denominational churches, has been given the Mission of spreading the Gospel message to the lost and making disciples of all mankind. As we embrace this Mission and commit our finances to it, we can be sure God will bless us abundantly financially and in every way. Don't allow this abundance to scare you, and surely don't allow it to corrupt your heart, but use it wisely as a good steward of Jesus Christ.

Money's Purpose

"At the moment I have all I need—and more! I am generously supplied with the gifts you sent me with Epaphroditus. They are a sweet-smelling sacrifice that is acceptable and pleasing to God. And this same God who takes care of me will supply all your needs from his glorious riches, which have been given to us in Christ Jesus." Philippians 4:18-19 (NLT)

The church at Philippi was a devoted financial supporter of the Apostle Paul, as he went forward sharing the Gospel, making disciples, and establishing new churches. Paul told them, *"As you know, you Philippians were the only ones who gave me financial help when I first brought you the Good News and then traveled on from Macedonia. No other church did this"* (Philippians 4:15, NLT). The church in Philippi had committed to using the blessing of the Kingdom, which God had entrusted them with, for the work of their King, which Paul was aggressively doing. Now, Paul assures the people of the Philippi church that God will provide everything they need! In fact, all the riches of God were available to them through Christ Jesus! As the church in Philippi used their financial resources for the furtherance of God's Kingdom, they would find themselves thoroughly blessed financially and in every way by their Heavenly Father.

The finances God blesses us with have a purpose! We are to diligently use our finances to advance the Kingdom of our King! As we do this, we can be certain we will lack nothing! God will find new and meticulous ways to abundantly bless us! God will bring us blessings from places we have never considered, and in ways we may have never thought possible. God is not limited in the ways in which He is able to bless His children! All the wealth of the Kingdom is for the children of the King! And, the King's children should be busy with the work of their Father! That includes using their blessings to purposely advance the Kingdom; supporting Kingdom work.

Now, as the children of God we should be moving in the wisdom of God. This means we should allow the Holy Spirit to direct us in how we use the money we have been entrusted with back into the Kingdom. Be sure, the devil will bring along false teachers and scoundrels, who will want the blessings that God has given us, but we are to invest that money into ways that will build the Kingdom. We are warned, "*My dear friends, don't believe everything you hear. Carefully weigh and examine what people tell you. Not everyone who talks about God comes from God. There are a lot of lying preachers loose in the world*" (1 John 4:1, MSG).

We must evaluate carefully, and judge righteously, as we take the financial blessings God has given to us and invest them into the growth of the Kingdom. As well as into those who are actually out there diligently and purposely laboring to spread the Gospel message and making disciples of men and women. If they are not methodically involved in the work of the Great Commission, we would be wise to invest our resources elsewhere. This truth includes us personally as well; our labors should always involve the work of spreading the Good News about Jesus Christ to others and making disciples. I have nothing against humanitarian work, but the children of the King (every born-again believer) are called not just to humanitarian work, but to the work of the Great Commission! Yes, we are to remember the poor, but what an injustice we do to them if we only feed their stomachs with food and neglect to share the Gospel message with them. As the representatives of Christ, we must do both!

One man who truly understood the purpose of God's blessing and the source of wealth was George Muller. Muller was born in 1805 and lived to be 92 years old. During that time, he served as an evangelist, pastor, and a missionary, bringing the Word of God to 42 countries. Muller is known for his great faith, which brought in great wealth that was used for the advancement of God's Kingdom.

In 1834, Mueller founded The Scripture Knowledge Institute for Home and Abroad. The Institute accomplished many great things for the Kingdom of God, but the contribution for which it was (and still is) best known was its work with orphans. Muller led the Institute in building five homes for orphans. Muller would house and feed over 10,000 orphans in his life. Muller never took a loan, he never did a fundraiser, he never directly asked anyone for money, and in the last years of ministry he never took a salary. Yet, he was never in lack, nor were the orphans he provided for. Muller learned to rely on the Lord, and through the course of his life prayed in millions of dollars to finance all the ministry he did.

Mueller's faith, that his prayers for financial means would be answered, was rooted in the sovereignty of God and God's goodness. When faced with a crisis of having the means to pay a bill he would say, *"How the means are to come, I know not; but I know that God is almighty, that the hearts of all are in His hands, and that, if He pleased to influence persons, they will send help."* That is the root of his confidence: God is almighty, the hearts of all men are in his hands, and when God chooses to influence their hearts they will give.

Once when Muller was confronted with the possibility of losing a piece of property that he wanted for the next orphanage he was preparing to build, he said, *"If the Lord were to take this piece of land from me, it would be only for the purpose of giving me a still better one; for our Heavenly Father never takes any earthly thing from His children except He means to give them something better instead."* Muller was confident in the sovereign goodness of God, and not only God's ability to supply, but His desire to supply abundantly for His children.

The key to Muller's success, and the reason he had the abundant blessings of the Kingdom at his disposal, can be found in his own words, when he said, *"The first great and primary business to which I ought to attend every day was, to have my soul happy in the Lord."* Thus, the Bible says, *"Take delight in the Lord, and he will give you the desires of your heart"* (Psalms 37:4, NRSV). As we delight in the Lord, we will find the resources of the Kingdom at our fingertips to do all God has placed in our hearts to do. Delight in God – not in money! Have faith in His Word – do not fear that He will fail you! *"Steep your life in God-reality, God-initiative, God-provisions. Don't worry about missing out. You'll find all your everyday human concerns will be met. Give your entire attention to what God is doing right now, and don't get worked up about what may or may not happen tomorrow. God will help you deal with whatever hard things come up when the time comes"* (Matthew 6:33-34, MSG).

Jesus tells a story that illustrates how the blessings of the Kingdom have been given over to the servants of the Kingdom (which are the children of God) so that they may have the means to do the work of their King without financial lack. Jesus tells of a wealthy businessman going away on a long trip, but before he leaves, he calls three of his employees (servants) and entrusts each of them with a certain amount of money to do business on his behalf while he is gone. To one of his employees he gave five bags of gold, to the second he gave two bags, and to the third he gave one bag. Each of his employees were well provided for financially, but each was provided for with the purpose of doing their employers (masters) business.

Eventually the businessman returned and began to settle accounts, He called the three employees he had trusted to represent him and his interest while he was gone. The first and second servant were both found to be wise servants, having doubled the money they were entrusted with, and, they were both awarded accordingly. But the third employee was a completely different case. Instead of taking the money he had been entrusted with and doing business for his employer, he took the money he was given and hid it away; frightened that he may lose it in a bad investment. The employer (master) was greatly displeased. In this tale, which Jesus shares, the master was furious, and he tells his servant, *"That's a terrible way to live! It's criminal to live cautiously like that! If you knew I was after the best, why did you do less than the least? The least you could have done would have been to invest the sum with the bankers, where at least I would have gotten a little interest"* (Matthew 25:26-27, MSG).

Money has its rightful place in the life of God's children. In the Kingdom of God, for the servant/child of God, money should never be an issue. And the children of God should never be afraid of money, nor should they ever love it, but they should take their Master's money and wisely invest it, doing business on their Master's behalf, until He returns to settle His accounts.

Prosperous

"Great is the Lord, who delights in the welfare of his servant."
Psalms 35:27 (NRSV)

God delights in blessing His children, which includes blessing them financially. Just as an earthly father takes delight in giving his children good things, so our Heavenly Father delights in giving His children the best of things. God's not looking to withhold financial blessings from us, but He's not going to give us things that will cause us harm. Jesus attempts to drive this point home, when He says, *"You parents—if your children ask for a loaf of bread, do you give them a stone instead? Or if they ask for a fish, do you give them a snake? Of course not! So if you sinful people know how to give good gifts to your children, how much more will your heavenly Father give good gifts to those who ask him"* (Matthew 7:9-11, NLT).

As a father myself, these verses speak volumes of truth to me. I love my children and can honestly say I delight in giving them good things. It brings me joy to be able to provide for my children. If they desire something, and it's not something that'll hurt them, I'm delighted to give it to them. They don't have to earn it or deserve it, I'm ready to give it to them simply because they are my children and I love to give good things to them. My children find themselves blessed by default, because of their position as my child. Regardless of how good they behave, they will always remain my children, which in-turn means they will always have my favor and love, and I will always delight in giving them good things!

Now, if I, who am a sinner by nature, would do this for my children, how much more will my Heavenly Father, who is righteous by nature, do for me? Would my Father in Heaven hold back the good things of His Kingdom from me? Would He desire to see me struggle with and worry about finances? Or, would He freely bless me, and delight in doing so? Be certain, God is good, and will never give us something that would hurt us or draw us away from Himself; that's what the devil does. God is a good Father, who seeks to prosper His children. He prospers us so we can do what He's called us to do, free from the worries that financial instability brings. Even beyond this, our Father in Heaven simply delights in seeing His children blessed. Without the blessing of our Father, we could never be a blessing to this world. Money and prosperity are part of that blessing, and because you are His child through Jesus Christ, you are qualified to freely receive all the blessings of the Kingdom, which include, but are certainly not limited to, financial blessings.

To fully prepare ourselves to receive the blessings of our Father, we must recognize God as our Father and Heaven as our home. If we see this world as our home, and then attempt to equate God as a Father, we'll never fully grasp who we are in relationship to the Creator of the Universe. We may call Him our Father, but for all intents and purposes, we will continue to view Him as a far-off God, with whom we have a limited relationship. And, if our relationship with our Heavenly Father remains limited, so will our ability to receive the abounding blessings that He delights in showering upon His children! Never forget the words of David, when he said, *"You show me the path of life. In your presence there is fullness of joy; in your right hand are pleasures forevermore"* (Psalms 16:11, NRSV). It is only through an intimate relationship with our Father that we will remain close enough to Him to live a life full of joy, where our Father is able to freely lavish His goodness upon us.

Love and Trust

"Then Jesus looked around and said to his disciples, 'How hard it will be for those who have wealth to enter the kingdom of God!'" Mark 10:23 (NRSV)

One day, when traveling with His disciples, Jesus comes upon a wealthy young businessman. The young man appears to be both respectable and sincere in his conversation with Jesus. He is concerned about his eternal soul, and so he asked the Master what he must do to inherit eternal life. The Bible is clear that Jesus holds no hostility towards the young man because he has wealth but looks upon him with a loving countenance. Jesus refreshes the young man's mind about the commandments, which the young man feels he has not failed in, and then, Jesus speaks to the issue of his wealth. Jesus does not condemn him for having wealth, this is not the issue, for Jesus would have other noted followers who had attained wealth, such as: Lazarus, Nicodemus, and Joseph of Arimathea. The problem wasn't the wealth the young man possessed; the problem was that the wealth had seeped into his heart. It is because of this, when Jesus challenges him to give his money away to the poor, he is unable to do it. The young ruler didn't understand where his wealth had come from, and that giving it away at the word of the Master would have resulted only in greater blessings of every type.

> "There is nothing wrong with men possessing riches. The wrong comes when riches possess men."
>
> Billy Graham

The young man in our story perceived money from the perspective of the world system, and therefore handled it as such. The Apostle John warns us against following the pattern of this world, when he writes, *"Don't love the world's ways. Don't love the world's goods. Love of the world squeezes out love for the Father. Practically everything that goes on in the world—wanting your own way, wanting everything for yourself, wanting to appear important—has nothing to do with the Father. It just isolates you from him. The world and all its wanting, wanting, wanting is on the way out—but whoever does what God wants is set for eternity."* (1 John 2:15-17, MSG). It is not only money that can seep into the hearts of God's children, but anything they would dare to value more than the One true God who has redeemed them.

God has no issue in blessing His children with money, His issue is with them loving that money and seeking it over their relationship with Him. God loves us so much He was willing to give up everything for us! *"For God so loved the world that he gave his one and only Son, that whoever believes in him shall not perish but have eternal life"* (John 3:16, NIV). He simply wants us to love Him with this same love; as any parent would. When Jesus is asked about the greatest commandment of all, He says, *"Love the Lord your God with all your heart, all your soul, all your mind, and all your strength"* (Mark 12:30, NLT). As we draw close to the Lord and He increases our finances, we must be certain that money and riches do not become our focus. The Scriptures admonish us on the subject of wealth by saying, *"If your wealth increases, don't make it the center of your life"* (Psalms 62:10, NLT).

Too often God's children put their trust in money, instead of in their Heavenly Father. Both rich and poor alike can be guilty of trusting in money. The amount of money they have dictates to them what they can and cannot do for the Lord. When God speaks to them, they do the seemingly wise thing (according to worldly practices) and consult their bank account to make sure they can financially do what God has called them to do. The Scriptures tells us, *"Those who trust in their riches will fall, but the righteous will thrive like a green leaf"* (Proverbs 11:28, NIV). God's children must put their confidence in their God, and not in their money! And, the only way we can put our trust into God is to have and maintain an intimate relationship with Him. It is in this intimate relationship we will find ourselves thoroughly blessed in every way, and at the same time riches and wealth will have no control over us, nor will they find a place of affection in our hearts.

Hudson Taylor, who spent 51 years in China advancing the Kingdom of God, once said, *"Many Christians estimate difficulties in the light of their own resources, and thus attempt little and often fail in the little they attempt. All God's giants have been weak men who did great things for God because they reckoned on His power and presence with them."* Learning to trust in God, regardless of what our financial means may appear to be to the natural eye, brings us to a place where we're able to go beyond any boundary that may lie in our way, so that we may do great things for our King!

Application and Self-Reflection

1. How do you determine what you spend your money on?

_____

_____

_____

2. What role do the Scriptures play in how you use your finances?

_____

_____

_____

3. How do you currently view the connection between the money you have and the purpose to which God has called you?

_____

_____

_____

4. How can you avoid the dangers of allowing money to seep into your heart?

_____

_____

_____

5. How can you be certain to wisely use the blessings God has entrusted to you?

_____

_____

_____

6. What does it mean to you to abide in the presence of God?

_____

_____

_____

7. How can you be sure to do this?

_____

_____

_____

Chapter 3

Paths of Blessings

"Blessed are all who fear the Lord, who walk in obedience to him. You will eat the fruit of your labor; blessings and prosperity will be yours." Psalm 128:1-2 (NIV)

The main sanctuary of the church I pastor is cooled by two 15-ton units; living in southeast Texas makes air conditioning a very important necessity for most. Both units were originally purchased back in 1986, but in recent years they both had to have a lot of repairs to keep them going. In 2016 we had come to the point where it seemed as though the A/C repair man was out at the church grounds on a regular basis, but by the grace of God they continued on. One evening we had an electrical storm that cause a power surge, which took out both units. Both units were completely ruined.

Not only was the price tag to replace both units a hefty one, it was one we couldn't come close to affording. I called the company that holds the church's insurance policy to see if they would possibly help with the expense of replacing them. Knowing both units were 30 years old I wasn't sure what they would be willing to do. The insurance company sent several inspectors out to look at the units, and the damaged cause to them by the power surge. When they finished their investigation, they decided to pay the total bill to replace both units! Even though both units were 30 years old they didn't prorate the amount they were willing to pay, but instead, paid the total cost (minus a $1,000 deductible) to replace both units!

God had led us monthly to use our financial resources for the work of the Great Commission, and without hesitation He was faithful to provide financial help when we needed it. God gave us great favor in the eyes of the insurance company, who willingly replaced both units. We found that as we sought the advancement of God's Kingdom that He was faithful to richly provide for all we needed, so that we could continue to be generous on every occasion. God is always good!

> "So instead of fields, buy souls that are in distress, as anyone is able, and visit widows and orphans, and do not neglect them; and spend your wealth and all your possessions, which you received from God, on fields and houses of this kind. For this is why the Master made you rich, so that you might perform these ministries for him."
>
> The Shepherd of Hermas

Delighting in the Lord

"Blessed is the one who does not walk in step with the wicked or stand in the way that sinners take or sit in the company of mockers, but whose delight is in the law of the Lord, and who meditates on his law day and night. That person is like a tree planted by streams of water, which yields its fruit in season and whose leaf does not wither—whatever they do prospers." Psalm 1:1-3 (NIV)

God, as a loving Father, is always looking to bless His children; to provide them with the ways and means to do all He has called them to do. To experience the fullness of God's blessings, including financial blessings, the children of God must learn to delight in their Father as He delights in them. The word delight in the psalm above means to desire something valuable. To delight in the Lord means to recognize the great value in being close to the Lord, and to desire that above all else. God delights in us, and desires to be with us so much that He was willing to die for us.

Delighting in the Lord brings us to a place where we long for Him above all else, and we see the pricelessness of a close relationship with Him. When we delight in the Lord we can say as the psalmist, *"Whom have I in heaven but you? And earth has nothing I desire besides you"* (Psalm 73:25, NIV). To delight in the Lord is to desire Him above all else, and when this desire is real, we will actively seek after Him, and, when we seek Him with all our heart, we will find Him!

When we find the giver of all good things, we will have all good things! Those who delight in the Lord find themselves blessed in every way; including financially! As God's children, we should seek His face and not merely His hand. *"My heart says of you, 'Seek his face!' Your face, Lord, I will seek"* (Psalm 27:8, NIV). To seek God's hand is to seek His blessings; to seek His face is to seek an intimate relationship with Him.

All of God's children want to be blessed by their Heavenly Father, and, their Father wants to bless them. The problem is, when we seek after the gift, we miss the Giver. If we miss the Giver, we will never have the gift, and will live in confusion and disappointment, wondering why God is not providing for us or answering our prayers. On the other hand, when we seek the Giver, we also find the gifts. This is why the person who delights in the Lord will find themselves blessed financially and, in every way, prospering in all they do!

When we delight in the Lord, desiring and seeking Him above all else, we find our heart begins to match His heart; we desire the same things that our Father does. The heart of God longs for the lost souls of this world to be saved, it wants to see committed men and women discipled, and the works of the devil upon this earth destroyed. When our heart's desires match that of our God, we can be certain they will be given to us! *"Take delight in the Lord, and he will give you the desires of your heart"* (Psalm 37:4, NIV). Remember, the blessings of the Kingdom are for the children of the King, so that they may be fully provided for, without financial hinderances, to do the work of their King in this world!

Money is a tool the children of God use to do the work of their Father, as they represent their homeland here in this life as ambassadors of Christ. The Apostle Paul wrote, *"So we are ambassadors for Christ, since God is making his appeal through us; we entreat you on behalf of Christ, be reconciled to God"* (2 Corinthians 5:20, NRSV). As ambassadors we have the resources of our homeland to represent and do the work of our King in this world. We do not trust in money, nor do we seek it, but we have it at our disposal to do the work of our King while we are in this world. *"Praise the Lord. Blessed are those who fear the Lord, who find great delight in his commands. Their children will be mighty in the land; the generation of the upright will be blessed. Wealth and riches are in their houses, and their righteousness endures forever"* (Psalm 112:1-3, NIV). Wealth and riches belong to those who delight in their Lord, who desire

53

and seek Him, and long to see His will accomplished in this world!

When Solomon became king over Israel, the Lord appeared to him and asked what he wanted. Solomon could have asked for wealth and riches, but he did not. Rather, Solomon asked for a heart of wisdom to rule the people of God. Solomon, like the Lord, wanted to see the people of Israel ruled justly and righteously. Solomon's heart matched up with the heart of God. Because Solomon didn't seek riches and wealth, but sought the heart of his God, he gained both. The Lord told him, *"Since this is your heart's desire and you have not asked for wealth, possessions or honor, nor for the death of your enemies, and since you have not asked for a long life but for wisdom and knowledge to govern my people over whom I have made you king, therefore wisdom and knowledge will be given you. And I will also give you wealth, possessions and honor, such as no king who was before you ever had and none after you will have"* (2 Chronicles 1:11-12, NIV). Delight in the Lord, allowing your heart to match up with His, and you will have the wealth of your King to do the work of your King!

To delight in the Lord, is to trust in the Lord. The child of God should never trust in the wealth or riches of this world, they are merely tools to do the work of their King. We must place our trust in the Lord alone, seeking Him and His will above everything else! Jesus said, *"But strive first for the kingdom of God and his righteousness, and all these things will be given to you as well"* (Matthew 6:33, NRSV).

Seekers of God and His Kingdom find what they are looking for, and when they find that intimate relationship with the Lord, they also find that all their needs are met. The seekers of God need not strive to gain riches and wealth, the Lord freely gives both to them. They do not seek money but find they have it available to them to use in their pursuit to advance the Kingdom of God. Seek the Blesser above the blessing and you will have both! Seek the blessing and not the Blesser and you will find neither!

As we delight in the Lord and His Word, we follow after His word, obeying His commands and living by His precepts. In doing this we draw closer to the Lord, learning to love and adore Him. We find an intimate relationship with our Father in Heaven, for we have sought His face and not His hand, and in doing so, we receive the benefits of both. But the Bible warns us, if we forsake the commands and precepts of the Lord and choose to live life according to our own desires, that we will be drawn away from the Lord. We will not prosper in the things we do, for the face of the Lord will be hid from us. For, as obedience out of faith draws us into a more intimate relationship with the Giver of all good things, a life of sin out of rebellion pulls us away from the Giver of all good things.

The Bible says, "*Indeed, the Lord's hand is not too short to save, and His ear is not too deaf to hear. But your iniquities have built barriers between you and your God, and your sins have made Him hide His face from you so that He does not listen*" (Isaiah 59:1-2, HCSB). Again, it says, "*The one who conceals his sins will not prosper, but whoever confesses and renounces them will find mercy*" (Proverbs 28:13, HCSB). If you're trapped in sin, or if you're indulging in it, and think you can hide it, understand, it is destroying your relationship with your Father in Heaven. It is driving you further and further apart. Understand also, sin is not limited to things such as drunkenness and adultery, it also included living in fear, responding to God's word with doubt, and the uncontrolled words of slander and gossip that spew from the mouths of many of God's children.

If we allow sin to have place in our lives, we will miss the intimate relationship our Father in Heaven wants to have with us, which means we will also fail to experience the blessings and provision of His hand. If you are trapped in some pattern of addictive sin, and you don't feel as if you can escape on your own, ask a mature brother or sister in Christ to help you. If you need help don't be afraid to ask, remember, "*As iron sharpens iron, so one person sharpens another*" (Proverbs 27:17, NIV).

Pictures of Blessings

"Every generous act of giving, with every perfect gift, is from above, coming down from the Father of lights, with whom there is no variation or shadow due to change." James 1:17 (NRSV)

Our God is a good God, and He takes delight in blessing His children! Our Father's goodness doesn't change over time but remains constant throughout time and circumstance. Our good Father lavishes His children with things that will bless them and enables them to be a blessing to the Kingdom. Those blessings may appear differently in the life of each of His children. What appears as a good gift to someone living in New York City, may be extremely different from someone living in a small village in Niger, Africa. The blessings may be different, but they come from the same source with the same purpose; to bless the receiver, so that they may be a blessing. We must understand that the gift of wealth comes packaged differently, but should be expected and received with the same spirit of humility, regardless of our geographical location, or the packaging the wealth is wrapped up in.

Throughout the Scripture we find the Lord blessing His people with wealth in a variety of ways. Many times, we only perceive wealth as coming by means of a large some of currency, which will be punctiliously delivered to our doorstep. Though it is not beyond God's ability to bless us with wealth in this manner, seldom does He package the gift of wealth in this way. It is for this reason that it can be easy to overlook God's blessings or to even forsake them. Let's look at three pictures of how the Lord blessed His children with wealth in the Scriptures. We will look at the landowner, the goat rancher, and the farmer.

Picture the Landowner

In the eighth chapter, of the Book of 2 Kings, we read about the Prophet Elisha and a woman from Shunem who showed great kindness to the prophet. The Shunammite woman built a room for the prophet to stay in whenever he was in town. Looking to repay her kindness the prophet inquires of what may be done for her. Gehazi, the servant of Elisha, tells the prophet that the woman has no child and that her husband was too old to do so. The prophet determines that the woman should be blessed with a son, and according to the prophet's word, she is.

The woman continues to show kindness to the prophet and their friendship continues to grow. Once, before a time of great famine in Israel, Elisha warns the Shunammite woman of the oncoming disaster, and instructs her to leave, so that she and her family will be spared from this great time of hardship. The woman heeds the words of the prophet and leaves. Through the course of time she returns to her home, but she finds her home and land had been taken by someone else.

The woman goes before the king to petition him to have her home and land returned to her. At the same time the woman comes before the king, Gehazi, the servant of Elisha, had just finished telling the king the story of how Elisha had raised the woman's son back to life after a farming accident. The king is amazed at the story and asked the woman if the story was true; she acknowledged that the story is indeed true. The king then shows the woman great kindness and favor, commanding that not only her home and land be returned to her, but any money that was made from the sale of crops harvested from the land would have to be returned to her as well.

God had uniquely positioned the women to receive His financial blessing. He placed all the pieces of the puzzle in place and led the Shunammite woman to petition the King of Israel at the perfect time. God's financial blessings are not hindered by time and circumstance, and He can make those blessings abound to us in His perfect timing and in His perfect way!

Picture the Goat Rancher

In the book of Genesis, we read about a man named Jacob, and we see another way in which God found to bless one of His children with wealth that transcended the direct delivery of a large pile of money. Jacob was the son of Isaac and had acted deceitfully in seeking the blessing of his father, which Isaac intended to give to his eldest son Esau. Esau was greatly angered when he learned that Jacob had received the blessing from his father. Jacob fears for his life and flees from the presence of his brother to the land of his mother's family. On his way there, Jacob stops for the night at a place he will name Bethel. It is here that the Lord appears to Jacob in a dream, and it is here that Jacob begins his relationship with the God of his fathers. After Jacob awakes from his dream he declares, *"If God will indeed be with me and protect me on this journey, and if he will provide me with food and clothing, and if I return safely to my father's home, then the Lord will certainly be my God"* (Genesis 28:20-21, NLT).

God would indeed protect and provide for Jacob as he entered the home of his uncle Laban. It is while Jacob is with his uncle that he will marry Leah and Rachel and spend over twenty years serving his uncle by carrying for his flocks. Laban was pleased with Jacob's work, for the Lord blessed all Jacob did, which meant that Laban was being richly rewarded as his herds increased.

To secure Jacob's continued service Laban strikes a deal with Jacob in which Jacob will be given all the speckled or spotted sheep, every dark-colored lamb and every spotted or speckled goat from Laban's flocks. It is at this point that Jacob will witness the Lord greatly increase his wealth, as the livestock that was to be yielded to Jacob increased drastically beyond all the other livestock of Laban. God was increasing Jacobs wealth by causing the speckled and spotted sheep, every dark-colored lamb and every spotted or speckled goat to be born. Wealth came to Jacob packaged in the form of livestock.

When Jacob prepared to depart Paddan Aram and return to the country of his father Isaac, he told Leah and Rachel, *"Your father has cheated me by changing my wages ten times. However, God has not allowed him to harm me. If he said, 'The speckled ones will be your wages,' then all the flocks gave birth to speckled young; and if he said, 'The streaked ones will be your wages,' then all the flocks bore streaked young"* (Genesis 31:7-8, NLT). He then tells them of a dream he had, *"In breeding season I once had a dream in which I looked up and saw that the male goats mating with the flock were streaked, speckled or spotted. The angel of God said to me in the dream, 'Jacob.' I answered, 'Here I am.' And he said, 'Look up and see that all the male goats mating with the flock are streaked, speckled or spotted, for I have seen all that Laban has been doing to you. I am the God of Bethel, where you anointed a pillar and where you made a vow to me. Now leave this land at once and go back to your native land"* (Genesis 31:10-13, NLT).

God had protected Jacob from the deceitful hand of his uncle and directed him in the path by which wealth would be added to him. This wealth did not come in the form of gold and silver, nor was it in the form of any kind of currency, but it came in the form of livestock. God brought Jacob to a place of wealth by causing certain colored livestock, that was to be yielded to him, to greatly reproduce.

The vehicle by which the Lord brought blessings to Jacob was livestock. We must recognize the vehicle by which God is attempting to bring us the blessing; allowing Him to direct us into the paths of prosperity He has determined for us to receive from. Recognizing the vehicle will ensure that we do not reject or neglect God's blessings because they come packed differently than we may have anticipated.

Picture the Farmer

When the children of Israel were freed from their captivity in Egypt, the Lord gave them instructions on how they should live once they came into the land He had promised to give them. In these instructions were precepts the Lord had set forth on how the Israelites were to tend the land. God set up a sabbatical year, which was to be every seventh year, in which the children of Israel were not allowed to plant seed nor to harvest anything the land had produced.

When we consider the consequences of neither planting seed nor harvesting the produce of the land, but leaving it totally at rest, it can easily be seen how a person who is dependent on what the land produces for their family's survival may become a little nervous. Not only would they have to go every seventh year without harvesting anything the land produced, but the following year would also put them at peril, for since they had not sown any seed, they would have no harvest to reap. God puts their hearts and minds at ease when He tells them, *"But you might ask, 'What will we eat during the seventh year, since we are not allowed to plant or harvest crops that year?' Be assured that I will send my blessing for you in the sixth year, so the land will produce a crop large enough for three years. When you plant your fields in the eighth year, you will still be eating from the large crop of the sixth year. In fact, you will still be eating from that large crop when the new crop is harvested in the ninth year"* (Leviticus 25:20-22, NLT).

God, in His faithfulness, would supernaturally provide an abundant crop for the children of Israel who followed His precepts regarding the sabbatical year in faith. God was able to cause their crops to produce three times as much on the sixth year, providing all they would need, and even going beyond what they would need to make it through. God provided a

61

blessing for His people by causing their crops to supernaturally produce.

God is able to bless His children with provision in a variety of ways. For the farmer in the jungles of Guatemala He can cause their crop to supernaturally produce. For the stockbroker in New York the Lord can cause their stocks to greatly increase in value. For the goat rancher in Tanzania the Lord can cause their herds to reproduce far above the normal rate. The blessings of provision and finances can come to the Lord's children in variety of ways, so, we should throw-off any preconceived idea about how the Lord will bless His children with the gift of finances. Allowing Him to lead us, as we walk in faithful obedience, having the works of our hands blessed and prospered. The Scriptures assure us, *"Blessed are all who fear the Lord, who walk in obedience to him. You will eat the fruit of your labor; blessings and prosperity will be yours"* (Psalm 128:1-2, NIV).

Leaning on God

"Trust in the Lord with all your heart; do not depend on your own understanding. Seek his will in all you do, and he will show you which path to take." Proverbs 3:5-6 (NLT)

To walk in obedience, on the path the Lord directs us, is going to take a lot of trust! It can be very difficult to walk in a path we don't understand, or one we didn't plan out for ourselves. But it's along the path our Lord has prepared for us that we will find all the blessings of God, which have been laid up for us to receive by faith.

One of the reasons many of God's children never receive the fullness of the blessings He has prepared for them to use in the work He has called them to do, is that they draw back from the path the Lord has prepared for them to walk, never allowing it to unfold as the Lord had intended for it to. In Psalms 106, the psalmist recounts the journey of Israel out of the captivity they were subjected to in the land of Egypt. He speaks of the great wonders God did for them, and how He brought them through the sea safely and destroyed the Egyptian army. The psalmist tells us that when this happened, they praised God and believed His promises. But, through the course of time they would face other challenges and hardships, and it would be in this time that they would forsake God's plan for them in favor of something else, something that perhaps seemed easier or better. The psalmist wrote, *"But they soon forgot what he had done and did not wait for his plan to unfold"* (Psalm 106:13, NIV).

God has planned a path for each of us to walk, and along that path are many trials and challenges, which tempt us to take another path or to take things into our own hands. When we become anxious and don't allow God's plan for us to unfold as it was meant to, we miss out on the blessings and provision of God. The financial blessings of God can only be found on the path He has laid out for us. For it is on this path that we will need the resources of God to fulfill the purpose of God. When we take another path, not allowing God's plan to unfold as it should, we miss the financial blessings God had prepared for us to receive, because we failed to walk in faith, trusting God's way over our own. Leaning on God's understanding leads us to the financial blessing we'll need to do the work of our God here in this life. Leaning on our own understanding moves us away from those blessings, and away from the glorious future God had planned out for us.

Olaudah Equiano was a child of God whose path led him through hell (where he refused to stop) and into a life of prosperity and wealth. Olaudah was born in Nigeria; at age 11 he was kidnapped, along with his sister, and sold to European slave traders. Eventually Olaudah was purchased by Michael Pascal, a sailor in the Royal Navy. After gaining a certain amount of respect from his master, Olaudah was sent to England where he gained a basic education. It was during this time that he became a follower of Jesus.

Olaudah would begin to use the Scriptures to shape the perspectives of others regarding slavery. In his early twenties, Olaudah, was able to purchase his freedom. He would eventually author a book that recounted his experiences as a slave, which sold well and went through many editions. The revenue from the sale of his book allowed Olaudah to live independently, devoting much of his time to the campaign against slavery in England. Olaudah became a supporter of the London Missionary society; a Christian organization committed to advancing education and Christianity overseas.

Olaudah's path was not an easy one, but it led him to a place of wealth and influence where he was able to impact the world he lived in for the Kingdom of his Lord. Walking the path God puts us on, and prospering financially along the way, requires that we not lean upon our own understanding, but instead, make a conscious choice to trust God, believing that He loves us and will surely lead us in paths of prosperity for His name sake.

Application and Self-Reflection

1. What does it mean to trust and lean on the Lord?

_____

_____

_____

2. How might someone actively and purposely do this?

_____

_____

_____

3. How can you recognize the path God has prepared for you to walk?

_____

_____

_____

4. How can you effectively walk that path in faith?

_____

_____

_____

5. What might hinder you from walking the path God has for your life?

_____

_____

_____

6. How can this hindrance be overcome?

_____

_____

_____

7. What are some ways you could use the wealth God has given you to advance His Kingdom?

_____

_____

_____

Chapter 4

Faith Receives

"And without faith it is impossible to please God, because anyone who comes to him must believe that he exists and that he rewards those who earnestly seek him." Hebrews 11:6 (NIV)

In September of 2008, Hurricane Ike ripped through the Gulf Coast, causing an estimated $37.6 billion in damage. My brother who didn't have a job, and was going through a rough season, was living with us at the time. My wife was working on Galveston Island for an optical company, but when Ike came through, the damage to the eye clinic was severe enough that they made the decision not to reopen. Now, both my brother and wife were without a job. Things were tight, but God continued to supply for all our needs.

One evening, at a Wednesday night service, as we were preparing to take up the offering, the Lord spoke to my heart, and told me to empty out my wallet into the offering basket and He would fill it up. My wife and I had always given a minimum of ten percent of whatever God had blessed us with, and, just because she was without a job and my brother was living with us, who was also without of a job, made no difference. We had already given ten percent, in addition to giving an offering that was designated to go directly to the foreign missionaries that we help to support.

Now, I had planned on putting something in the offering that night, but I had no intentions of emptying my wallet out. But I had learned to listen to the Lord and trust Him with the money He had entrusted to me. So, just as the Lord had told me to do, I emptied out every dollar that was in my wallet. That evening, as we were headed back home, my wife delivered some welcoming news. She told me that a lady in our church had given her a check for us. The lady told my wife that as she was sitting in church the Lord spoke to her and told her to write us a check for a specific amount, which she had done. The amount was nearly double what I had put in the offering! True to His word, God had filled my wallet up!

An act of faith, in response to the word God had spoken to my heart, caused the blessing of God to become a reality in my life that evening. Faith receives the blessing of God! Faith is the hand that opens the window of Heaven, allowing the riches of God's goodness to overflow our lives. Faith cannot be manufactured through positive thinking or behavior adjustment. True faith comes from our Lord and is birthed through a relationship of love and intimacy with our Heavenly Father; this kind of faith is never left disappointed!

Living Under the Law

"Therefore there is now no condemnation for those who are in Christ Jesus. For the law of the Spirit of life in Christ Jesus has set you free from the law of sin and of death." Romans 8:1-2 (NASB)

Here Paul addresses the way we are made right with God, not right and wrong behavior as defined by the Scriptures. Paul is not telling the church in Rome that they are free to live in any manner they want. What Paul is telling them, is that there is a new way to be made right with God. For all those who have made a choice to call on the name of Jesus for salvation, believing that God raised Him from the dead, surrendering their lives to His lordship, they have been made free from the penalty that sin brings.

This means we no longer have to justify ourselves before God; Jesus has done that for us. The Scriptures declare *"For no one can ever be made right with God by doing what the law commands. The law simply shows us how sinful we are. But now God has shown us a way to be made right with him without keeping the requirements of the law, as was promised in the writings of Moses and the prophets long ago. We are made right with God by placing our faith in Jesus Christ. And this is true for everyone who believes, no matter who we are"* (Romans 3:20-22, NLT).

The blessings of God, which includes monetary blessings, are for those who have been made right with God through Jesus. The blessings of God are no longer distributed on a *this-for-that* system. God's blessings are based upon our relationship with Him; they are by grace and not by works, it is for this reason that no one can boast about deserving or earning them. Yet, it is possible for the child of God to miss the blessings of God, because they try to earn them. When we try to merit ourselves by our own deeds of righteousness before God, we miss out on the blessings that have been made freely available to us by faith through Jesus Christ.

God told the children of Israel before they entered the Promised Land *"Look, today I am giving you the choice between a blessing and a curse! You will be blessed if you obey the commands of the Lord your God that I am giving you today. But you will be cursed if you reject the commands of the Lord your God and turn away from him and worship gods you have not known before"* (Deuteronomy 11:26-28, NLT). The children of

Israel would be blessed according to their works. The blessings they received, both monetary and non-monetary were directly tied to their behavior.

Many followers of Christ try to justify the blessings they receive by the commandments they follow. They feel if they're good enough, God will richly bless them, and, if they miss the mark too badly, they will also miss the blessing. Unfortunately, the Bible makes it clear, *"For whoever keeps the whole law and yet stumbles at just one point is guilty of breaking all of it"* (James 2:10, NIV). Therefore, if we attempt to justify ourselves worthy of receiving the blessings of God based upon our behavior, we are sure to find ourselves always coming up short.

The beauty of receiving through our relationship with God, and not by our works, is that our relationship with God also provides a source of strength by which we receive the power of God to live a holy and righteous life. It is from an intimate relationship with God that our faith grows, enabling us not only to freely receive the blessings of God, but also to live a life free of the practices of sin, which always bring death and destruction to those who live in them. The financial blessings of God (along with every blessing of God) cannot be purchased, nor is it possible to earn them, they must simply be received by faith, through Jesus Christ.

Faith Expressed

"Melchizedek blessed Abram with this blessing: 'Blessed be Abram by God Most High, Creator of heaven and earth. And blessed be God Most High, who has defeated your enemies for you.' Then Abram gave Melchizedek a tenth of all the goods he had recovered" Genesis 14:19-20 (NLT)

Abraham, throughout the Bible is referred to as a friend of God. He was told by God to leave his home country, and to follow the Lord into unknown territory. He was given no specific destination, but he was assured that God would bless him. So, Abraham (Abram at the time) packs up all he owns and takes a leap of faith. Abraham developed a relationship with the Lord, one in which he clearly recognized that the blessing of God was upon his life.

Abraham's relationship with God can clearly be seen when the Lord appears to him when he is in Mamre. Abraham is sitting in the tent door when he sees three angelic beings. Immediately, he jumps to his feet and runs out to meet them. Abraham is excited to receive his visitors, he has water brought to wash their feet, and quickly prepares to serve them a delicious meal. Abraham's actions towards the angelic beings are indicative of someone who has a personal relationship with another, which can also be seen in the Lord sharing His plans with Abraham concerning the destruction of Sodom. Abraham had a personal and intimate relationship with God.

It is through this relationship that the financial blessings, which overwhelmed the life of Abraham would flow. Abraham recognized the blessing of God upon his life. So, when Abraham's nephew Lot is taken captive by King Kedorlaomer of Elam, and Abraham and his men rescue him and the other captives and is offered certain spoils of war by the king of Sodom, Abraham refuses. Abraham declares he will take nothing from him, for he didn't want the king of Sodom to be able to brag that he was the one who made him rich. Abraham understood the blessing of God was with him and had brought him great wealth.

It is during this encounter that Melchizedek comes out to Abraham and blesses him, and, Abraham gives him a tenth of all the goods he had recovered. Abraham doesn't do this because he's required to, nor does he do it because he wants God to bless him. Abraham gives this tithe based on his relationship with God, and, his understanding that he was blessed already. This act of giving is nothing more than an expression of Abraham's inward faith. It is the same faith that moved Abraham out of his old life, and into the life of blessing and prosperity that God had given him.

> "Faith, mighty faith, the promise sees, and looks to God alone; Laughs at impossibilities, and cries it shall be done."
>
> Charles Wesley

Faith expressed is faith that receives! True faith is more than a mere emotional feeling. Rather, it is a supernatural force that propels the Christ follower to action, in response to the word of God. This supernatural force of faith is secure in an unwavering belief that God is good, and that His love for the follower of Christ will never waver. For true faith is birthed from an intimate relationship with our Lord.

Tithing

The first example of tithing is found in the life of Abraham, and eventually it would become part of the law given by Moses. In response to the blessing of God the people were to offer a tenth of their increase, and in doing so, they would be assured of God's continued blessing. Failure to give a tithe was seen as stealing from God. The Scriptures declare, *"Will a mere mortal rob God? Yet you rob me. But you ask, 'How are we robbing you?' In tithes and offerings. You are under a curse—your whole nation—because you are robbing me. Bring the whole tithe into the storehouse, that there may be food in my house. Test me in this, says the Lord Almighty, and see if I will not throw open the floodgates of heaven and pour out so much blessing that there will not be room enough to store it"* (Malachi 3:8-10, NIV).

Here we clearly see God operating on a this-for-that system. This was the underlining principle for the entire Old Covenant, which was given to Israel through Moses. It was a Covenant which Abraham did not live under. Under the Old Covenant a person was made ceremonially right with God based off of what they did, which in-turn, either qualified them or disqualified them to receive the blessings of God. The people had to be right with God, in accordance to the agreement they had made with God (The Old Covenant), to receive anything good from God. This was not the case with Abraham, nor with Isaac or Jacob, for a quick glance through the Book of Genesis clearly shows their multiple failures, and yet, God continued to bless them financially. Why? Because, they were blessed apart from the Law, based on their relationship with God and not their works. Because they were not aware of the Law, they never tried to justify themselves by it. They were simply blessed because of the free grace of God, which abounded in their lives because of their relationship with God.

Now, under the New Covenant, we have been made right with God through Jesus Christ alone! The Scriptures say, *"For it is by grace you have been saved, through faith—and this is not from yourselves, it is the gift of God— not by works, so that no one can boast"* (Ephesians 2:8-9, NIV). Because our sin has been taken away through the works of Jesus Christ, by the grace of God alone, we are now forever right with God! And because we are right with God, we are free to receive the blessings of God apart from our works. The Scriptures say, *"Blessed are those whose transgressions are forgiven, whose sins are covered. Blessed is the one whose sin the Lord will never count against them"* (Romans 4:7-8, NIV). If we will only depend upon the grace of God, and not our own works, to receive His blessings, we will surely see our lives overwhelmed by those blessings; just as Abraham did apart from the Law.

Consider further what the Apostle Paul goes on to write to the church in Rome, when he says:

> It was not through the law that Abraham and his offspring received the promise that he would be heir of the world, but through the righteousness that comes by faith. For if those who depend on the law are heirs, faith means nothing and the promise is worthless, because the law brings wrath. And where there is no law there is no transgression. Therefore, the promise comes by faith, so that it may be by grace and may be guaranteed to all Abraham's offspring—not only to those who are of the law but also to those who have the faith of Abraham. He is the father of us all (Romans 4:13-16, NIV).

All the blessings we receive from God can never by merited by the deeds of our hands, they must be received by simple faith, which has been birthed and nurtured inside our hearts in response to God's word and our intimate relationship with Him.

Now, we must firmly grasp the understanding that right and wrong has not changed throughout time. Coveting your neighbor's belongings is just as wrong now as it was when Moses received the Law. The difference now is twofold: First, we are not judged on our behavior, but on our relationship with Christ. *"But when the kindness and love of God our Savior appeared, he saved us, not because of righteous things we had done, but because of his mercy. He saved us through the washing of rebirth and renewal by the Holy Spirit"* (Titus 3:4-5, NIV). This means the blessing of God flows freely to us by faith through Jesus Christ.

Second, we have been given the Spirit of God, which gives us strength to live a holy and righteous life. Something those living under the Old Covenant did not have. *"I will give you a new heart and put a new spirit in you; I will remove from you your heart of stone and give you a heart of flesh. And I will put my Spirit in you and move you to follow my decrees and be careful to keep my laws"* (Ezekiel 36:26-27, NIV). The Spirit of God gives us the strength of God to live a life free of the deeds of sin. The extent to which we are able to exercise this power, that lives inside us, will testify to the intimacy we share with our Heavenly Father. For the closer we are to our Lord, the stronger the Spirit will be inside us, and, the holier our lifestyle will be.

Right and wrong did not change from the Old Covenant to the New Covenant; they will forever remain the same. Under the Old Covenant it was wrong to lie and steal, and now that the Old Covenant has been done away with, it's still wrong to lie and steal. That hasn't change! Just as under the Old Covenant it was right to give a tenth (or tithe) of all God had increased you with, and, to give other offerings on top of that, it's still right today under the New Covenant. Jesus said, *"I tell you the truth, until heaven and earth disappear, not even the smallest detail of God's law will disappear until its purpose is achieved.*

So if you ignore the least commandment and teach others to do the same, you will be called the least in the Kingdom of Heaven. But anyone who obeys God's laws and teaches them will be called great in the Kingdom of Heaven" (Matthew 5:18-19, NLT). Right and wrong have not changed! What has changed is the way we are declared right with God. *"I do not treat the grace of God as meaningless. For if keeping the law could make us right with God, then there was no need for Christ to die"* (Galatians 2:21, NLT). We are now declared right with God through Jesus Christ, and, if we are right with God through Jesus Christ, we are eligible to receive all of His goodness and blessings through Jesus Christ as well!

Tithing, just as the choice not to lie or steal, is an act of faith. Yes, they are also commandments to be followed by the servants of the Lord, nonetheless, they will only be followed by *"faithful"* servants; that is servants who are full of *"faith"*. Faith is a supernatural force that is both birthed and nurtured inside our deepest being, founded on our relationship with the Lord. And, it is this faith that moves us to tithe and give offerings, to abstain from lying and adultery, to choose to willingly submit our lives to God, doing the things that please Him, and, it is this same faith that causes us to receive the blessings of God! Only by faith can we receive from God!

Tithing is an outward expression of an inward faith. It is not the means by which we gain the financial blessings of God; that is done by Jesus. Rather, tithing under the New Covenant, is an expression of a believer's inward faith, which has been birthed from their relationship with the Lord, and it is by this faith that they receive the blessing.

Give Freely

Once we recognize the financial blessings of God, that rest upon us because of Jesus Christ, we will understand that we are free to generously give, so that the Kingdom of our Lord may advance across this world! Freedom from the Law makes us free to give generously, for we understand the blessing that is on us, and, we understand the purpose of that blessing. The Apostle Paul in his writings to the church in Corinth said:

> Remember this: Whoever sows sparingly will also reap sparingly, and whoever sows generously will also reap generously. Each of you should give what you have decided in your heart to give, not reluctantly or under compulsion, for God loves a cheerful giver. And God is able to bless you abundantly, so that in all things at all times, having all that you need, you will abound in every good work. As it is written: 'They have freely scattered their gifts to the poor; their righteousness endures forever.' Now he who supplies seed to the sower and bread for food will also supply and increase your store of seed and will enlarge the harvest of your righteousness. You will be enriched in every way so that you can be generous on every occasion, and through us your generosity will result in thanksgiving to God. This service that you perform is not only supplying the needs of the Lord's people but is also overflowing in many expressions of thanks to God. Because of the service by which you have proved yourselves, others will praise God for the obedience that accompanies your confession of the gospel of Christ, and for your generosity in sharing with them and with everyone else (2 Corinthians 9:6-13, NIV).

Paul uses the analogy of a farmer to help us understand how the followers of Christ should give:

1. Reaping Requires Sowing.

We must understand if we are to reap a great crop we'll need to sow generously; meaning, the advancement of our Lord's Kingdom is going to have to be a financial priority. Unfortunately, too many people take this verse to be a means by which they can *"earn money"* from God. They believe by giving money they will get money; their heart is still set on a this-for-that system. This has caused disappointment and misunderstanding of how God works in the hearts and minds of many followers of Christ, and, it has hindered the relationship our Lord desires to have with His followers. The harvest we look to reap must always be made up of the souls of mankind. The followers of Christ shouldn't be looking to get rich by giving the money away God has entrusted them with. Instead, they are to use that money as good stewards to further the expansion of the Kingdom.

2. Giving is a Matter of the Heart.

Giving is a heart matter, not a Law matter. Our giving is to be done in faith that springs up out of a deep love for our Lord. God wants His children to enjoy giving; He doesn't want to force them to give as He had to do under the Old Covenant. Consider this, *"Before the coming of this faith, we were held in custody under the law, locked up until the faith that was to come would be revealed. So the law was our guardian until Christ came that we might be justified by faith. Now that this faith has come, we are no longer under a guardian"* (Galatians 3:23-24, NIV). The Law was like a guardian that makes a child do the right thing, but faith brings a maturity in which the follower of Christ doesn't have to be treated like, nor should they behave like, a child. With the faith of Christ living inside us, we should no longer have to be made to give ten percent and other offerings, we should do it willingly and cheerfully.

Love moves us to give and commit our finances to the work of the Lord, so that the Kingdom of our Lord may continue to advance. Amy Carmichael, a long-time missionary to India, put it this way, *"You can always give without loving, but you can never love without giving."* Under the Law, and still in many churches today, people were made to give or were guilted into it. But this is not what God wants! God wants His children to give freely in faith, with a joyful heart out of love for Him! Under the Law you can give, and you can receive, but it is the way of a child; it is not to be the way of the Christ follower. *"When I was a child, I talked like a child, I thought like a child, I reasoned like a child. When I became a man, I put the ways of childhood behind me"* (1 Corinthians 13:11, NIV).

3. God Looks to Abound His Blessing to His Children.

Our God is able to bless His children abundantly! We have no need to earn His blessings, for He gives them freely to the followers of Christ. God's grace extends beyond the mere replacement of the finances we use to further His Kingdom. God is able to greatly multiply our finances, beyond what we have spent to further His Kingdom, so that *in all things at all times, having all that we need, we will abound in every good work.* God doesn't want His children held back from doing His work because of a lack of financial resources. He is ready to abundantly bless us, so that we may continue to be a great blessing to the work of the Kingdom upon this earth! Money is given to us as a tool to be used for the work of our Lord; it is not to be horded, nor cherished, but used so that we may *abound in every good work* for the glory of our King! When the children of God change the way they think about money, and how God multiplies it to them, they'll never again experience a lack of it!

4. We Must Generously Scatter Seed.

To further illustrate how the follower of Christ is to give, Paul quotes from the Book of Psalms when he says, *"They have freely scattered their gifts to the poor; their righteousness endures forever."* The child of God is compared to a farmer, who does not sow sparingly, but rather scatters his seed everywhere. We are to have a generous heart that allows us to scatter our finances for the work of the Kingdom. The results of scattering our finances for the Mission of Christ is that our righteous works will endure forever! As we generously give to the work of the Kingdom, we share in the eternal reward given to the winner of souls!

Jesus said, *"Do not store up for yourselves treasures on earth, where moths and vermin destroy, and where thieves break in and steal. But store up for yourselves treasures in heaven, where moths and vermin do not destroy, and where thieves do not break in and steal"* (Matthew 6:19-20, NIV). Add to this, *"Those who have insight will shine brightly like the brightness of the expanse of heaven, and those who lead the many to righteousness, like the stars forever and ever"* (Daniel 12:3, NASB). What our Lord values and desires are the souls of mankind! As such, we would be wise to adjust our value system, so that it lines up with that of our God! God doesn't need money; the abundance of the world belongs to Him! When we give a tithe or an offering, we're simply returning to Him what He's entrusted to us. When we give in hopes of receiving money it reveals a serious character flaw in our heart. Our heart's desire should match that of our King's heart. Money is easy, and our God is ready to freely and abundantly give it to His children, but His children would be wise to give their heart a check-up; ensuring their motives for giving are in line with the heart of their God.

Scatter your money generously to aid in the work of the Great Commission! Understand, God is willing and able to supply you with all the money you need, and He does this apart from anything we may do. We don't earn His financial blessings; He freely and abundantly gives them to us through Jesus our Lord. So, set your heart on reaping an eternal reward of souls for your Lord! Look for a return of souls when you sow your finances towards the work of the Kingdom, and not the return of mere money. The world seeks after money and financial reward, but we are not of this world! We are the children of God, and we seek after the things of the Kingdom! Remember the words of our Lord, "*So don't worry about these things, saying, 'What will we eat? What will we drink? What will we wear?' These things dominate the thoughts of unbelievers, but your heavenly Father already knows all your needs. Seek the Kingdom of God above all else, and live righteously, and he will give you everything you need*" (Matthew 6:31-33, NLT).

5. What we Plant and what we Harvest are not the Same.

Paul makes it clear that God provides seed, and, brings a harvest of righteousness. Clearly, we see that we are not harvesting more seed, but rather we are harvesting righteousness. Seed here is equal to the money we scatter for the sake of the Kingdom. God increases our seed, which means He gives us more financial resources. In fact, God goes so far in this increase that it gives us an excess amount of finances. The phrase *"increase your store of seed"* literally means that God will multiply your seed (money) that is to be used for sowing. God looks to multiply our finances, so that we can generously sow into the work of the Kingdom.

We must never forget; we are children of the Kingdom and we are to live with a Kingdom mindset. Our goal is not to merely accumulate a large bank account, dedicated to providing us with a life of ease. Our aim is to advance the message of the Gospel, to make disciples of all nations, and to destroy the works of the devil! God is ready and willing to multiply our finances; we must be wise with those finances; using them in a way that brings glory to our King! We are people of purpose, and that purpose has been defined by our King! *"Do not be ashamed, then, of the testimony about our Lord or of me his prisoner, but join with me in suffering for the gospel, relying on the power of God, who saved us and called us with a holy calling, not according to our works but according to his own purpose and grace. This grace was given to us in Christ Jesus before the ages began"* (2 Timothy 1:8-9, NRSV).

As children and servants of the Lord, the harvest we seek to reap is not money; that is only the seed Paul speaks of. The harvest we look to reap is one of righteousness; it is the redeemed souls of mankind! We are to use our seed (or money) in a way that brings about a harvest of souls.

We are not harvesting seed (money); that would be foolish! Our seed (money) is freely given to us by our God. We are to use that seed (money) in a manner that will yield a righteous harvest of souls! Therefore, God is so eager to make us rich in every way, because as we give generously towards the work of the Kingdom, our Lord will be glorified, and people will be saved! The wealth of the Kingdom is for the children of the King, and it is freely given, so that they may be abundantly supplied, as they set their hearts and hands to do the work of their King!

The Destroyer of Faith

"See to it that no one fails to obtain the grace of God; that no root of bitterness springs up and causes trouble, and through it many become defiled." Hebrews 12:15 (NRSV)

How is it that the child of God could miss out on the grace of God that brings the blessing of financial abundance? By allowing the root of bitterness to spring up in their heart.

The phrase *root of bitterness* signifies a poisonous plant. Bitterness, as a source of poison, destroys the faith by which we are to receive the grace of God, preventing the financial blessings God desires to bestow upon His children from being realized. By embracing jealousy and resentment, we allow bitterness to fill our hearts, and this cancer eats away at the blessing of God.

When the follower of Christ looks upon the blessings of others and becomes jealous and begins to resent others who are experiencing the financial blessings of God, they allow bitterness to spring up in their heart, and it is this bitterness that poisons the grace of God. Too often church leaders, and Christians in general, look on the blessings of others and resent their brothers and sisters in Christ for the abundance their Father in Heaven has given them. Fear tells them God can't, or won't, do it for them, and, once they embrace this lie, they allow the blessing of God to be stolen from their life.

We should celebrate the blessings of our brothers and sister in Christ, knowing we share the same generous Father, and just as He has blessed them abundantly, He will do the same for us. The root of bitterness is a poisonous cancer that prevents the grace of God from abounding in our lives, so, be aware of it!

Understand that bitterness grows in the soil of fear, so allow the love of God to fill your heart, and, choose to show that love to others by your deeds of kindness and generosity. Nourish the soil of your heart, so that the faith of Christ springs up and fills every part of your being, bringing the blessings of God to full maturity in your life!

Nurturing the Soil of your Heart

We must be diligent to guard our heart and to keep it properly nourished, so that the love of God may abound there. How can we both guard and nourish the soil of our heart? By praising God!

The Prophet Hosea wrote, "*Ephraim is a trained heifer that loves to thresh; so I will put a yoke on her fair neck. I will drive Ephraim, Judah must plow, and Jacob must break up the ground. Sow righteousness for yourselves, reap the fruit of unfailing love, and break up your unplowed ground; for it is time to seek the Lord, until he comes and showers his righteousness on you*" (Hosea 10:11-12, NIV). Judah literally means praise, so, when we praise God, we are plowing the field of our heart, ensuring that the soil is good ground, and breaking up any bitterness that attempts to take root.

Remember the blessings of God in your life and praise Him for them! Focus on what God has done for you, and is doing, so you won't trip over what He's doing in the lives of others. Praise Him for what He's done and for who He is! Let His praise continually be on your lips, and you will eat the fruit thereof, as the blessings of God overflow your life. Never forget, *"From the fruit of their mouth a person's stomach is filled; with the harvest of their lips they are satisfied. The tongue has the power of life and death, and those who love it will eat its fruit"* (Proverbs 18:20-21, NIV).

Seasons

"I will make them and the region around my hill a blessing; and I will send down the showers in their season; they shall be showers of blessing." Ezekiel 34:26 (NRSV)

As we grow in the Lord, walking the path He lays out for us, we find that we pass through various seasons. These seasons often represent stages of growth and maturity in our relationship with Christ, and in the ministry He has called us to. If we keep the right perspective as we go through these seasons, we are certain to reach the place where the blessings of God come down on us like showers of rain.

Frederick Douglass was born into slavery in the 1800's. Forced to face the horrors and injustices of slavery, Douglass refused to allow bitterness to take root in his heart. He eventually escaped from the bonds of slavery and became a powerful and inspirational voice in the abolition of slavery in America. Douglass recounts, in his darkest hours of slavery, how he held on to a conviction that *"slavery would not always be able to hold me within its foul embrace."* Douglass saw the hand of

God leading him to a place of freedom, he said, *"This good spirit was from God, and to Him I offer thanksgiving and praise."*

In the midst of the most dreadful and darkest of places, Douglass made a conscious choice not to focus on where he was, but on where he was headed. He didn't resent others who had a better life then himself, but believed the blessing of God would ultimately overtake him. And eventually, that's exactly what happened. After escaping to freedom, Douglass wrote the first of four books in 1854 entitled *Narrative of the Life of Fredrick Douglas, an American Slave*, which became a best seller and was reprinted many times. Douglass would travel the world preaching about the evil and injustices of slavery, and all the while God prospered him financially, and gave him favor and fame worldwide, which he used to destroy the works of the devil.

Perhaps your situation isn't great, perhaps its similar to Fredrick Douglass, and the idea of God blessing you with financial abundance seems like nothing more than a fairy tale. If you'll make a conscious choice to maintain the right attitude and perspective, keeping the praise of God on your lips and in your heart, the faith of Christ will grow in your life, and you will indeed experience the abundant blessings of your God!

Application and Self-Reflection

1. How have you seen your faith grow over the years?

_____

_____

_____

2. How has your faith been challenged as it applies to your financial situation?

_____

_____

_____

3. How might a lack of faith be hindering the financial blessing of God from being fully realized in your life?

_____

_____

_____

4. How could this hindrance be overcome?

_____

_____

_____

5. How do you feel when you look upon your brothers and sisters in Christ who have been blessed financially?

_____

_____

_____

6. Has bitterness found its way into your heart?

_____

_____

_____

7. If so, how can you repent of it and make your heart ready to receive the financial blessings of God?

_____

_____

_____

Chapter 5

Awareness of the Presence

"I can never escape from your Spirit! I can never get away from your presence!" Psalm 139:7 (NLT)

In 2013 I led a team of six people to Niger, Africa on a missionary trip. Once on the ground, we began to minster and share the Gospel. The population there is overwhelmingly Muslim, so the potential for Kingdom growth is fantastic. One of the things we were set to do there was to minister to a people group called the Gormanche. We were scheduled to host a youth rally in a village named Tamou. It was about an hour and a half ride to the village; to get there we traveled in two separate vehicles. Myself, two other team member, and a missionary friend traveled in one vehicle, and the remainder of the team followed us in a second vehicle.

We were almost to our destination, when the second vehicle flipped off the road as it went around the curve. Tragedy had struck us in the worst way possible that day. One team member died on the side of the road there, and two others were severely injured. The two team members who were injured needed emergency help, which Niger could not offer. Their injuries were life threatening and they needed to be brought back home on an air-ambulance immediately.

My wife, who was back in the U.S., contacted the insurance carrier we had contracted with for the trip, they informed her that we would need to pay $120,000 for the air-ambulance (the portion the insurance policy covered was very minimal). At the time the amount seemed overwhelming. In the midst of this tragedy we were facing, to hear we needed to come up with $120,000 was a bit overwhelming, and, the money had to be received within the next 24 hours. I remember I was standing in the hospital lobby when my wife told me this, and I immediately shared it with Kristen and Ben (our other team members). Ben and I quickly began to explore other possibilities of getting the ladies home, but Kristen looked up at us and said, *"That amount is nothing more than a penny to God!"* We knew what she said was true, so we repented of our thoughts, and called my wife back.

I told her to let everyone in the church know and to get the word out on social media. Immediately, when we decided to trust God to provide the money, things began to happen! Shortly after I hung up with my wife she called back and said the insurance company had contacted her and there was an air-ambulance in Dubai that was going to be empty on their return trip back to America. Because they were close by, and had no one scheduled to ride home with them, they were willing to discount the amount they normally would charge. On top of that, we had found favor with the insurance company, as many of the people in the office were following our story; with this the insurance company had also decided to help us out by further discounting the amount needed!

We started off needing $120,000 dollars for the air-ambulance, but now that amount had amazingly shrunk by $45,000! We now only needed to come up with $75,000 in twenty-four hours. Everyone in the church got involved in getting the word out, and several of the local news channels picked up the story. Money began to pour in from all over the country! The insurance company gave us another 12 hours to come up with the money. And within thirty-six hours the Lord had brought in $85,000!

We had enough to pay for the air-ambulance and the medical expenses that were incurred while in Niger. God had graciously provided for the $120,000 need in His own unique way!

The journey to receiving God's provision started with a leap of faith, a leap that recognized we were not alone; God was with us! This tragedy represents a moment in my ministry that I will never forget, for it was a moment I saw the hand of God move in the most miraculous ways. One of the ladies who had been injured in the accident had her back broke in five separate places, and God miraculously healed her back by the time she arrived home! Through it all, God was with us! We were never alone!

Power of the Presence

You will make known to me the path of life; In Your presence is fullness of joy; In Your right hand there are pleasures forever."
Psalm 16:11 (NASB)

Only when we abide in the presence of God will we experience the fullness of His blessing! God is the giver of the blessing. He is the One who overflows our cup! The Lord provides us with seed to scatter. He is the one who gives us the knowledge to gain wealth. It is the Lord who leads us in paths of prosperity for the sake of His name and His Kingdom. Because of this, we can easily see the importance of abiding in His presence at all times.

Yes, it is true, there is no where we can go to escape His presence. Yet, how often do we move through our daily lives unaware of His abiding presence that is with us? As daily challenges present themselves, do we consider that the creator of the Universe is with us? How often do we take into account the power of the Holy Spirit, which lives inside us?

A constant awareness of the presence of God is mandatory, if we wish to experience the fullness of His blessing! A conscious awareness exceeds a mere cognitive understanding of this truth. We can possess the intellectual knowledge concerning the facts of God's abiding presence, yet, go throughout our daily lives as if He were nowhere near. For many Christians, this is the reality they exist in.

> "The root-trouble of the present distress is that the Church has more faith in the world and the flesh than in the Holy Ghost, and things will get no better till we get back to His realized presence and power."
>
> Samuel Chadwick

They have a cognitive understanding of what the Scriptures declare about the presence of God, but they live their lives like God is on a planet far-far away.

We must live with a constant awareness that God is with us! We must understand we are never alone. The proof of this awareness is sure to be seen in our behavior. When we step into a bank, a church, or even a grocery store, our behavior is noticeably different then when we're home alone with our family. Why? Because we are aware of the differences in our surroundings, and the people whose presence we are in. Our awareness of the presence of others affects our behavior. If the awareness of mere mortals changes the way we behave, how much more should our awareness of the Lord's abiding presence change the way we live out our daily lives, and face the many challenges we are presented with?

A simple cognitive understanding does nothing to help us realize the blessing of God that has been given to us through Jesus Christ. But, a true awareness of our Lord's presence and His Holy Spirit that abides inside us, will dramatically change the way we live, and, the way we experience His abounding blessings!

Consider the words of our Lord, as recorded by the Prophet Isaiah, *"For I hold you by your right hand—I, the Lord your God. And I say to you, 'Don't be afraid. I am here to help you'"* (Isaiah 41:13, NLT). How near is our God to us? Close enough to hold our hand and walk with us through all the challenges of life! As we walk through this life holding the hand of our Heavenly Father, we can be certain that He will bless us and abundantly provide for us! How foolish it would be to become numb to His presence, pulling away from the One who loves us, and missing all the goodness of our gracious and generous Father!

We'll look at three examples from the Scripture that really highlight the importance of God's presence in living a blessed and prosperous life, and the need to be aware of that presence beyond a cognitive understanding.

The House of God

Jacob was the son of Isaac, the grandson of Abraham. Eventually God would change Jacob's name to Israel, and from Jacob would come the twelve tribes of Israel, for he would have twelve sons. But before that would happen Jacob would come to experience God in a way that few today ever do.

Jacob's journey begins as a farmer, who seizes a rather strange sounding opportunity when he buys his brothers birthright. Jacob was the twin brother of Esau; Esau came out first, and then came Jacob holding on to the heel of his brother. As the first born, the birthright ensured Esau would have all the privileges that the first-born son was to receive. But one day, Esau comes in extremely hungry and sees his brother's lintel soup, in his hunger, he agrees to trade his birthright for a bowl of Jacob's soup (apparently, he was VERY hungry).

Through the course of time their father begins to age, and there comes a point when he prepares to give a blessing to Esau. Now, this blessing was no small thing, and once spoken it could not be taken back. Jacob's mother learns of the father's intent, and desires for the blessing to be given to him. She conceives a plan to deceive the boys aging father into believing that Jacob was Esau. The plan works, and Jacob receives the blessing. When Esau learns of Rebecca's and Jacob's treachery, he is furious, and sets his heart on killing his brother. In fear, Jacob flees to the homeland of his mother. It will be on this journey that Jacob discovers a radical truth, which will forever change his life.

On his way to Harran, Jacob becomes tired and stops for the night. While he's sleeping, he has a dream in which he sees a stairway sitting on the earth, with its top reaching into Heaven, and the angels of God were going up and down on it. Above it all stood the Lord, who speaks to Jacob ensuring him that He will be with him and bless him. When Jacob awakes, he says, *"Surely the Lord is in this place, and I wasn't even aware of it!"* But he was also afraid and said, *"What an awesome place this is! It is none other than the house of God, the very gateway to heaven"* (Genesis 28:16-17, NLT)!

Jacob comes to the realization that God was there with him and he never knew it! Jacob was unaware of the presence of God. This is a truth for many of God's children today; they are unaware of God's presence. They have a cognitive understanding of the fact that God lives in them through the Holy Spirit, but they live their life out as if He were on a distant planet somewhere. They are not aware of the abiding presence of God that is always with them. Because of this, they miss out on the blessings that come from being in God's presence; for in the presence of the Lord is fullness of joy!

We must develop an awareness of the presence of God, if we want to live in the blessings of God! If we're unable to recognize the presence of God, how can we hope to receive the blessings of God? We understand from the Scriptures that the Lord is always with us, but we must develop an awareness of His abiding presence. When we have this awareness, it will change the way we behave, for we will understand, and our actions will testify to the fact that we are never alone!

God's in the House

The Ark of the Covenant represented the presence of God. It was just a small wooden box overlaid with gold. Inside this box rested the Ten Commandments, a pot of manna, and Arron's rod that had budded. The Ark was covered by what was known as the Mercy Seat. This was the place where the presence of God rested. Two long wooden poles were used by the priest to carry the Ark as they traveled through the wilderness, it was also often carried before them into battle, and it was carried before them as they crossed the Jordan River into the Land of Promise. The Ark was a powerful physical representation of the presence of God, which was abiding with the people of God.

When David became king of Israel, he set out to bring the Ark to Jerusalem. When the children of Israel had originally crossed over into the Promised Land the Tabernacle, which housed the Ark, was finally set up in Shiloh. But the Ark had been captured by the Philistines, and when it was returned it was never brought back to Shiloh, but eventually finds its new home in Gibeah. Now that David is king, he wants the Ark where he is, so he set out to retrieve the Ark. On the way back to Jerusalem, the Ark, which is being transported on a cart, is shaken and appears as if it may fall from the cart. Uzzah, a man traveling with David, reaches out his hand to steady the Ark, when he touches it the Lord strikes him dead. Only the priests were allowed to touch the Ark, and because of this act of irreverence God kills him.

David is terrified and unwilling at this point to move the Ark to Jerusalem, so, a decision is made to place the Ark in the house of Obed-Edom. While in his house, Obed-Edom experienced the blessings that comes from the presence of the Lord. The Bible says, *"The Ark of the Lord remained there in Obed-Edom's house for three months, and the Lord blessed Obed-Edom and his entire household. Then King David was told, 'The Lord has blessed Obed-Edom's household and everything he has because of the Ark of God'"* (2 Samuel 6:11-12, NLT).

The presence of the Lord brings the blessings of the Lord! For the New Covenant believer, we are a living breathing Ark of God! The Apostle Paul poses this question to the Believers in Corinth, *"Do you not know that you are God's temple and that God's Spirit dwells in you"* (1 Corinthian 3:16, NRSV)? The same question must be asked today! For if we truly understand that the Spirit of God is with us, this understanding is sure to affect the way we behave and the way we perceive every situation. An awareness of the presence of God is an absolute must, if we are to live in the fullness of His blessing!

Obed-Edom had the advantage of actually seeing the Ark of the Covenant in his home; it would have been difficult to ignore this fact. But for the follower of Christ, we must take it by faith, and, if we can bring ourselves to wholeheartedly believe this truth, we will surely experience the fullness of God's abounding blessings. Thomas, one of the original followers of Christ, refused to believe the report of Jesus' resurrection without seeing Jesus and feeling His scars; Thomas needed tangible proof. Jesus gave Thomas the proof he needed, but then He tells him, *"Because you have seen me, you have believed; blessed are those who have not seen and yet have believed"* (John 20:29, NIV).

Maintain a constant awareness that the Giver of all good things is with you; that you are always in the presence of the Lord Most High! If you can do this, you should expect to always be blessed and prospered by your Good Father who stands ready to generously bless you, so that in all things at all times, having all that you need, you will be able to abound in every good work!

A Heart After God

David is referred to by the Lord *"as a man after my own heart."* David surely made his share of mistakes, but despite them all, what separated him from his predecessor Saul, was his desire to be with God. David wanted the Lord near him, it is for this reason that he originally sets out to bring the Ark to Jerusalem, instead of returning it to the Tabernacle in Gibeah.

When David finally brings the Ark of the Covenant into Jerusalem, he sets up a tent next to his home to place it in. It is here that the Ark will remain until Solomon builds the Temple. This tabernacle, that the Ark was now resting in, would function very differently than the one Moses set up. There would be no animal sacrifices there, only sacrifices of praise. The tent would be surrounded by musicians assigned to play and offer sacrifices of praise to God twenty-four hours a day. The Bible says, *"David appointed the following Levites to lead the people in worship before the Ark of the Lord—to invoke his blessings, to give thanks, and to praise the Lord, the God of Israel"* (1 Chronicles 16:4, NLT). Here, at the tabernacle that David sets up, the Lord would be praised continually.

As we said, David was a man who made more than his share of mistakes, and he paid a hefty price for them. But he was also a highly blessed man. He came from herding goats to reigning over the nation of Israel as its king. God blessed David in every way, simply because David wanted to be in the presence of God. He was a man after the heart of God. And, it would be through praise, which turned his attention to the Giver of all good things, that David would find God's heart, and in-turn, live a blessed life that far surpassed any works of righteousness that he could have done.

Staying Aware

"O come, let us sing to the Lord; let us make a joyful noise to the rock of our salvation! Let us come into his presence with thanksgiving; let us make a joyful noise to him with songs of praise!" Psalm 95:1-2 (NRSV)

How do we maintain an awareness of the abiding presence of God, which surpasses a cognitive understanding? Praise Him! Speak to others about the goodness He has shown you! Stay continually aware of the Lord's presence by continually praising Him and thanking Him for all the wonderful blessings He has bestowed upon you, and, the glorious future you will one day have with Him!

As we praise the Lord, we will be focused on Him, and through this continuous action of reverence and love, we are certain to deepen our awareness of the Lord's presence. The Book of Hebrews says, *"Through him, then, let us continually offer a sacrifice of praise to God, that is, the fruit of lips that confess his name"* (Hebrews 13:15, NRSV). Praising the Lord keeps our eyes and attention focused on the presence of the only One who is able to abundantly bless us above all we could ask or think!

The Book of Acts tells of a time when Paul and Silas were ministering in Philippi and were taken prisoner by the town officials. Paul and Silas are placed in prison with both their hands and feet shackled; they are stripped of their clothes and beaten. But their circumstance didn't hinder their ability to come into the presence of the Lord and receive his blessing. The Scriptures record, *"Around midnight Paul and Silas were praying and singing hymns to God, and the other prisoners were listening. Suddenly, there was a massive earthquake, and the prison was shaken to its foundations. All the doors immediately flew open, and the chains of every prisoner fell off"* (Acts 16:25-26, NLT)!

Paul and Silas made a choice to seek God in the midst of this trial. They pray, and then they begin to praise God, in doing this, they turn their attention from the pain of their present circumstance and place it on their generous and gracious God! That brought them into the presence of God, where the blessings of God freely flow! The blessings of God were poured out upon them, and through this Jesus was glorified, and salvation came to the jailer and his household! The presence of God brought the blessing of God, which worked through Paul and Silas to further expand the Kingdom of their Lord! The blessings of God prosper us and gives us the ability to further expand our Lord's Kingdom; fulfilling the Great Commission He has handed down to us!

Consider the words of the psalmist, when he says, "*Worship the Lord with gladness; come into his presence with singing*" (Psalm 100:2, NRSV). And again, when he says, "*Enter his gates with thanksgiving, and his courts with praise. Give thanks to him, bless his name*" (Psalm 100:4). It is easy to see the key role that praise plays in our ability to stay aware of the Lord's abiding presence, and to both embrace and enjoy the blessings that are freely received simply from being in the presence of our Gracious Heavenly Father!

Application and Self-Reflection

1. What does it mean for God's presence to abide somewhere?

_____

_____

_____

2. What does it mean to you to have God's abiding presence with you?

_____

_____

_____

3. How should awareness of God's abiding presence affect your behavior?

_____

_____

_____

4. How have you welcomed God's presence into your everyday life?

_____

_____

_____

5. How have you neglected to show reverence for the abiding presence of God?

_____

_____

_____

6. What has been the outcome of your awareness, or neglect thereof, of the abiding presence of God?

_____

_____

_____

7. What are some things you could daily do to maintain an awareness of God's abiding presence?

_____

_____

_____

Chapter 6

Right Thinking

"And now, dear brothers and sisters, one final thing. Fix your
thoughts on what is true, and honorable, and right, and pure,
and lovely, and admirable. Think about things that are excellent
and worthy of praise." Philippians 4:8 (NLT)

How we think about God's blessings, the way in which the Lord provides for us, and the blessed life He intends for us to live is sure to have a direct effect on the way those things manifest in our lives. Wrong thinking about the blessings of God will hinder our ability to live a prosperous life for the sake of our Lord. On the other hand, when our thinking about prosperity and the blessings of God lines up with and come into agreement with what the Scriptures declare, those things will be free to abundantly fill our lives.

Several years ago, in general conversation with some of our church members, the topic of needing a bus arose. At the time there was no money to purchase a bus, or at least one that was in good working condition. I had already experienced the grace of God in providing financially for the work of the Kingdom in the past, and I knew that He could just as easily provide for this bus now. I expressed to those there that God would provide, by bringing a bus to us, and that we wouldn't need to go out and finance the purchase of one.

No small amount of time passed from that point, and then, on a Wednesday evening before service, a gentleman pulled up in a beautiful gleaming bus, got out and handed me the keys to it. Now, I knew he was coming, he had previously offered to buy the bus for the church (unsolicited) and suggested that he could bring it over before service on Wednesday night. This was just one more testimony in my life about how God both generously and freely gives His blessing to us. The bus was needed, and desired, but the family who purchased the bus for the church wasn't asked to do so, they freely offered (knowing they had been blessed by God for a reason).

Sometime after we had received the bus, one of the individuals who heard my original remarks about how God would provide the bus for us, told me, "*When you said that I thought you were a nut, but then low-and-behold someone pulls up to the church in a bus and hands you the key.*" This blessing had nothing to do with my works of righteousness, and everything to do with God's grace, and, an understanding of how that grace works. God's grace freely brings the blessings of God, which prosper us beyond anything we deserve, or anything we have earned. Right thinking about the abounding blessings of God opens the door for those blessings to freely abound in our lives!

> "Not until we have become humble and teachable, standing in awe of God's holiness and sovereignty, acknowledging our own littleness, distrusting our own thoughts, and willing to have our minds turned upside down, can divine wisdom become ours."
>
> J.I. Packer

Remember, "*Don't copy the behavior and customs of this world, but let God transform you into a new person by changing the way you think. Then you will learn to know God's will for you, which is good and pleasing and perfect"* (Romans 12:2, NLT). Free your mind from the lies of the enemy, the natural laws of this world, the ways of man, the limits of man, and your old thinking habits, and you can be certain that all the glorious blessings of God will overtake you!

Consciousness

"For I know my transgressions, and my sin is ever before me."
Psalm 51:3 (NRSV)

After David sinned with Bathsheba, and then had her husband killed, he is confronted by the Prophet Nathan. David's confession shows us the guilt he felt for doing wrong. He was fully aware that he broke the Law, and that sin was always on his mind; he couldn't escape the thoughts of his transgression. With his sin before him, he seeks the mercy of God. David writes, *"Purge me with hyssop, and I shall be clean; wash me, and I shall be whiter than snow"* (Psalm 51:7, NLT). And that's exactly what God does! The Prophet Nathan tells David, *"Now the Lord has put away your sin; you shall not die"* (2 Samuel 12:13, NRSV). David would pay a price for what he had done, but his sin was removed from him, and he was once again free to live a life full of God's blessings and favor.

The Apostle Paul makes it crystal clear, that for all of those who have trusted Jesus Christ for their salvation, choosing to follow Him, that they have been freed from the bonds of sin. *"There is therefore now no condemnation for those who are in Christ Jesus"* (Romans 8:1, NRSV). The child of God, can in no way, have condemnation placed on them; they are free! Our sins are never to be remembered by our Lord again, once they are washed from us by the blood of Jesus. The Scriptures declare, *"For as the heavens are high above the earth, so great is his steadfast love toward those who fear him; as far as the east is from the west, so far he removes our transgressions from us"* (Psalm 103:11-12, NRSV).

If God removes our sins, and forgets about them, so should we! We should no longer be conscious of our sin, but of the righteousness we have been given through Jesus Christ. We are naturally drawn to whatever we focus on. So, when the child of God is focused on sin and its penalty, their behavior will be reflective of their sin conscious. On the other hand, when God's children focus on the righteousness they have received through Jesus Christ, and the blessed life that comes with that righteousness, their behavior is sure to reflect their thinking. Not only will they willingly follow their Lord's commands, but they will do so in a state of blessedness that others will struggle to understand.

We must remain conscious of the right standing we have received through Jesus Christ, and how this right standing has opened the door for the blessings of God to freely and abundantly flow through. God's Word declares, *"Christ redeemed us from the curse of the law by becoming a curse for us—for it is written, 'Cursed is everyone who hangs on a tree'— in order that in Christ Jesus the blessing of Abraham might come to the Gentiles, so that we might receive the promise of the Spirit through faith"* (Galatians 3:13-14, NRSV).

The door that leads to the blessings of God was not opened by us, therefore, it cannot be closed by us! The door was opened by the righteous works of Jesus Christ; we simply receive access to it by faith, and not by our works or deeds! Because the level of God's blessings in our life hinge solely on faith, what we believe and how we think matters! If our past sin, and present failures, are always before us, and that is what we are thinking on, it will be seen in the way we live our life, which will surely seem absent from God's abundant provision, trapped in a life on habitual failure and sin. Yet, if we make a choice to focus on the works of Jesus, and the righteousness that has been passed to us through Him, our lives will abound in the provision of God and our behavior will be free from the destructive works of sin!

In the Old Testament Scripture, we find two men that serve to highlight the idea of right thinking, and how it opens us up to freely receive the blessings of God or causes us to miss the blessings. These men are Abraham and Mephibosheth.

Abraham

The Book of Genesis records the Lord calling out to Abraham saying, *"Leave your native country, your relatives, and your father's family, and go to the land that I will show you. I will make you into a great nation. I will bless you and make you famous, and you will be a blessing to others. I will bless those who bless you and curse those who treat you with contempt. All the families on earth will be blessed through you."* (Genesis 12:1-3, NLT).

Abraham (Abram at the time) responds in faith to the call of God, leaving all behind and following after the Lord. Notice the similarity to the call of God and Abraham's response, in relation to the call of Christ and the response of the first disciples. Both are called to leave what they knew and to blindly follow God, trusting in His goodness and grace, and, both respond in faith, leaving their old lives behind.

Abraham responds to God in faith 430 years before the Law was given to Moses. Abraham wasn't conscious of the Law or the penalty for breaking the Law. The only thing Abraham was conscious of was the promise God has spoken to him. A promise he responded to in faith. *"Abraham believed God, and God counted him as righteous because of his faith"* (Romans 4:3, NLT). Because Abraham responded to the word of God in faith, he was made right with God, and therefore eligible to freely receive all the blessings of God. The Scriptures declare, *"Clearly, God's promise to give the whole earth to Abraham and his descendants was based not on his obedience to God's law, but on a right relationship with God that comes by faith"* (Romans 4:13, NLT).

The Book of Genesis not only records how Abraham responded to the call of God in faith, but it also records the failures of Abraham. Twice, out of fear, Abraham lies about his relationship with his wife Sarah, and twice God comes to the rescue. In both cases the Law would have brought reprisal for Abraham's sin, but Abraham was not under the Law, he was under the grace of God. Therefore, God's response to Abraham's lies, that were told out of fear, was to deliver him out of the mess he had gotten himself into and bring him out of that mess financially blessed!

While in Egypt the Bible says, *"Abram acquired sheep and cattle, male and female donkeys, male and female servants, and camels"* (Genesis 12:16, NIV). Then again, when living in Gerar, Abraham acts in fear and deceives Abimelek about his and Sarah's true relationship, but God still rescues him from the situation he had gotten himself into and brings him out of that mess more financially blessed than when he went into it. Here the Bible says, *"Then Abimelek brought sheep and cattle and male and female slaves and gave them to Abraham, and he returned Sarah his wife to him"* (Genesis 20:14, NIV). In both cases the Law would have brought punishment, but because Abraham was not under the Law, but rather under grace, the blessings of God were free to abound to him apart from his works.

Because the Law was not given till long after Abraham was gone, he was never aware of its requirements. He never knew the blessings it promised for obedience, nor, the curses it declared for noncompliance. Abraham was only conscious of his relationship with God and the promise God had made to him. Abraham was never tempted to respond to God on a this-for-that system, for his relationship was one based on faith and not works of righteousness. Abraham's mind was never clouded by the idea that he had to earn the blessings of God by certain works, or by maintaining a certain behavior. For Abraham, all the blessings, the goodness, and favor of God were based on a relationship with God that prompted a heart of faith in Abraham, which caused him to receive the fullness of God's blessings into every area of his life!

Too many of God's children miss-out on the fullness of God's blessings today because they are conscious of the Law and its righteous requirements, more than they are conscious of the works of Jesus and the righteousness He has imparted to them. By the finished works of Jesus Christ, we are made right with God by faith, making the way to receive all the blessings of God! This is a fact we must stay conscious of!

The person who abounds in the blessings of God by faith, is certain not to be the same person who professes to know Christ and lives a life of indulgence in sin. For when we live in the blessings of God, trusting in the finished work of Jesus Christ, we are given a new heart that desires to live a life that is pleasing to God, and, we are also given the Spirit of God, which gives us the power to live such a life!

When we fail to stay conscious of the righteousness that comes through Jesus Christ and attempt to earn the blessings of God by our works of righteousness, we become conscious of the Law and the condemnation it brings. This is a path that is certain to lead us away from the fullness of God's blessings, and into a place of disappointment and frustration. An example of a person who failed to fully recognize the free grace that was offered to him, can be found in the story of Mephibosheth.

Mephibosheth

Mephibosheth was the son of Jonathan, and King Saul's grandson. Mephibosheth's story begins with a bond between Johnathan and David. In speaking of their relationship, the Bible says, *"Jonathan became one in spirit with David, and he loved him as himself. From that day Saul kept David with him and did not let him return home to his family. And Jonathan made a covenant with David because he loved him as himself. Jonathan took off the robe he was wearing and gave it to David, along with his tunic, and even his sword, his bow and his belt."* (1 Samuel 18:1-4, NIV).

The significance of what takes place here should not be lost with our modern understanding of friendships. At this point, Jonathan and David are much more than friends, they have entered into a covenant with one another that was unbreakable. This covenant had knotted the two men together as one, and, with this covenant each man carries the responsibility of caring for the other man's family as his own.

Through the course of time Jonathan and Saul would both die, and David would become king of Israel. When David becomes king of Israel, he remembers the covenant that he and Jonathan had made; for this covenant was an everlasting one. David says, *"Is there anyone still left of the house of Saul to whom I can show kindness for Jonathan's sake"* (2 Samuel 9:1, NIV)? It is for the sake of Jonathan alone that David seeks to show kindness to the descendants of Saul's house; specifically, to the children of Jonathan.

Through his inquiries, David learns that Jonathan still has a son living, his name is Mephibosheth. Mephibosheth was injured in an accident as a child and was lame in his legs because of this accident, he was living in the land of Lo Debar, in fear of what David might do to him, because he was a descendant of Saul. Mephibosheth was unaware of the covenant his father and king had made. A covenant that was about to bring him from a place of desolation to the table of the king!

David has Mephibosheth brought before him. I can only imagine the sheer terror that must have filled Mephibosheth's heart, knowing that he was the grandson of the man who once sat on the throne of Israel. Was David seeking him out to ensure the male descendants of Saul were all dead, so no one could make a claim to the throne…such thoughts were almost certain to have filled his imagination. When Mephibosheth is brought before David he bows down before him, and to his surprise finds the kind words of a king who looks only to bless him in every way possible. David says to him, *"Don't be afraid, for I will surely show you kindness for the sake of your father*

Jonathan. I will restore to you all the land that belonged to your grandfather Saul, and you will always eat at my table" (1 Samuel 9:7, NIV).

Mephibosheth is shocked, he can't understand why David would show kindness to someone like him; he sees himself as nothing more than a *dead dog*. What Mephibosheth failed to understand was that the kindness David desires to show him had nothing to do with him, and everything to do with the covenant that his father and king made long before he was ever born. David would graciously and abundantly bless Mephibosheth with more than he would ever need, and the blessing would come to him apart from anything he had done. Mephibosheth did not deserve to be blessed, but because of the covenant that was made, and by the grace of his king, Mephibosheth would freely and abundantly be blessed above anything he could have imagined!

This is a clear picture of what has been done for us! Very similar to David and Jonathan, our King and our Father entered into an everlasting covenant long before we were ever born. God now desires to show us kindness because of this covenant. Like David sought out Mephibosheth, God seeks out the followers of Christ to show them kindness for the sake of Christ. These followers are far from perfect and have done nothing to earn the blessing of God, but because of the covenant that was made, which they freely partake of through grace by faith, they are eligible to be abundantly blessed by their gracious God!

Yet, many of the followers of Christ have the same perspective as Mephibosheth, when he said, "*What is your servant, that you should notice a dead dog like me*" (2 Samuel 9:8, NIV)? Mephibosheth tried to reconcile the blessings David wanted to give him with who he was and what he had done, and the two didn't match up. This was simply because the two were not connected! The same is true for the followers of Christ today! All the blessings God looks to give us, including the financial ones, have nothing to do with our works or achievements. The blessings are based off of what Jesus has done, we simply receive them by faith, because of our relationship with Him!

Mephibosheth was only conscious of his failures and shortcomings. If we want to live in the abundance of God's blessings, we must be conscious of the work of Jesus! We must lose ourselves in thoughts of Christ and the righteousness He has given us, so that we may prepare ourselves to freely receive the all the blessings of God, which are based on the covenant that was made between our King and our Father! The blessings of God can only be freely received because of Jesus and through Jesus, they cannot be earned or merited in any way under the New Covenant! For it is not a covenant between us and God, but between God and Himself.

Think Blessed

"The blessing of the Lord makes a person rich, and he adds no sorrow with it." Proverbs 10:22 (NLT)

The way we think effects our ability to live a blessed life. So, if our thinking is not right, we need to make an effort to change it. Our mind must not be consumed with thoughts of punishment and reprisal, but rather, they should be consumed with thoughts of God's goodness and grace! Our focus should be on the finished work of Jesus, and not our failures and shortcomings. The way we perceive reward and punishment must line up with the New Covenant, if we truly want the blessings of God to overwhelm our lives!

Our thinking directs our behavior, if our thinking is wrong, our behavior is sure to follow suite. This is why the Lord says, *"Let the wicked forsake their ways and the unrighteous their thoughts. Let them turn to the Lord, and he will have mercy on them, and to our God, for he will freely pardon"* (Isaiah 55:7, NIV). If our thinking is filled with unrighteous thoughts, sooner or later our behavior will reflect those thoughts. But, if our thoughts are righteous, focused on the goodness and mercy of our God, we will behave in a manner that proclaims the righteousness of Jesus for the world around us to see.

There is a direct correlation between what we talk about and how we think. People who have the Spirit of God living in them, should find their conversations filled with talk of His goodness and love. The Apostle Paul, in his letter to the church in Ephesus, said, *"Don't be drunk with wine, because that will ruin your life. Instead, be filled with the Holy Spirit, singing psalms and hymns and spiritual songs among yourselves, and making music to the Lord in your hearts. And give thanks for everything to God the Father in the name of our Lord Jesus Christ"* (Ephesians 5:18-20, NLT). When our conversations are focused on the goodness of our God, our thoughts will be also! The Spirit of God will fill every part of our being, and it is the Spirit of God that will cause the blessings of God to manifest in our lives!

As Jesus ministered upon this earth, His message rested on the recurring theme of, *"Repent, for the kingdom of heaven has come near"* (Matthew 4:17, NIV). The word used to represent the concept of repentance is the Greek word *metanoeo*, which literally means *to think differently*. Jesus tells the Jewish people that they need to change the way they think about being right with God.

114

The basis for their relationship with the Lord rested on a this-for-that system known as the Law. This system revolved around the concept of them attaining their own righteousness through good behavior, and it was that same behavior that they felt qualified them or disqualified them from receiving God's blessings. The message Jesus had for the Jewish people required them to change the way they thought about being right with God, and in-turn, the way God would give His blessings to them.

Jesus didn't introduce a new God, just a new way of knowing and experiencing God! The God of the Old Covenant is the same God of the New Covenant! The difference is how we respond to God and how He responds to us. For the Jews of Jesus' day, and for the followers of Christ now, there had to be a change of thinking to experience the fullness of the blessing. The *this-for-that* system is no more! The New Covenant is an agreement between our King and our Father; we simply enter into it through faith. And it is in this same faith that we must abide to experience all the blessings of the Kingdom, including the financial ones.

Talk like a blessed person, and you'll think like a blessed person, which will lead you to behave like a blessed person! This takes faith, and it's only by faith that we receive the abundance of God's blessing! Refuse to be sin conscious, but rather stay conscious of the righteousness you have freely received from Christ Jesus! Let the goodness God has shown you be ever on your mind, and let it be spoken of by your lips! Think of the blessings and goodness of God, and not the disappointments, "*what ifs*", and failures, the enemy tries to flood your mind with! Think blessed and be blessed!!

Right Thinking About Money

"Teach those who are rich in this world not to be proud and not to trust in their money, which is so unreliable. Their trust should be in God, who richly gives us all we need for our enjoyment. Tell them to use their money to do good. They should be rich in good works and generous to those in need, always being ready to share with others." 1 Timothy 6:17-18 (NLT)

We must have our thinking about money founded in biblical truths, and not distorted by bad teachings and miss-understandings. If our thinking about money is off, so will be our ability to freely receive the financial blessing of God. Wrong thinking is like a cord that binds our hands and keeps us from receiving the blessing that God desires to give us.

Riches and wealth are simply tools the children of God can, and should, use to further the Kingdom of their Lord. God gives us riches and wealth so that all of our needs may be more than adequately supplied; there is nothing wrong with enjoying the wealth our Lord gives us. But, if our hearts are set only on consuming the riches and wealth God provides for us, we've got a serious problem. Right thinking about money brings the followers of Christ to a place where they neither fear money, nor do they love it, but simply use it as a tool while passing through this life.

John Chrysostom, was one of the most celebrated preachers of early Christianity, he once wrote:

> *The temporal goods are but an appendage to the spiritual ones; they are so vile and trifling in comparison with these, however great they may be. Let us not therefore spend our energies on them, but regard their*

acquisition and loss with equal indifference, like Job who neither clung to them when present, nor sought them absent. On this account riches are called chrēmata [utilities], so that we should not bury them in the earth but should use them rightly.

A clear understanding of money, and its place in the life of the Christ follower, can free our minds of wrong thinking and make the way for us to experience the abundance of God's financial blessings.

In 2017, Derek Car became the highest paid NFL quarterback in history, signing a five-year deal worth $125 million dollars. When asked what he was going to do with the money, after making some joking comment about going to Chick-Fil-A, he said, *"The first thing I'll do is I'll pay my tithe, like I have since I was in college when I was getting $700 on a scholarship check; that won't change."* He went on to say, *"The exciting thing for me, money wise, is that this money is going to help a lot of people...I'm thankful it's in our hands because it's going to help not just people in this country, but a lot of countries around the world."*

When the followers of Christ have their thinking about money lined up with the Scriptures, they won't love, nor will they fear it, but they will freely receive it and use it for the glory of their King and the advancement of His Kingdom around the world!

Application and Self-Reflection

1.   When you consider the possibility of having wealth and riches how does it make you feel?

_____

_____

_____

2. Describe how your thoughts and feeling about having wealth and riches line up with the Scriptures, or how they fail to.

_____

_____

_____

3. How would you describe your relationship with God?

_____

_____

_____

4. Do you have a relationship with God that mirrors Abraham or Mephibosheth?

_____

_____

_____

5. What does it mean to you to be righteousness conscious, rather than sin conscious?

_____

_____

_____

6. How do you believe the two types of consciousness could either help or hinder the financial blessings of God from being fully realized in your life?

_____

_____

_____

7. How can you stay focused on the righteousness Jesus has imparted to you?

_____

_____

_____

Chapter 7

Hands That Prosper

"However, we don't want to offend them, so go down to the lake and throw in a line. Open the mouth of the first fish you catch, and you will find a large silver coin. Take it and pay the tax for both of us." Matthew 17:27 (NLT)

Upon arriving in Capernaum, Peter is approached by those charged with collecting the Temple tax. It had long been required of every Jewish adult male to pay a tax of two-drachma to help support the maintenance done on the Temple. Jesus, not wishing to cause offense in this matter, is agreeable to pay the tax. But, where would the two-drachma come from? Would Jesus take up a collection? Would money rain down from Heaven? Would it come from a special fund they had set back?

The Lord would provide the money to pay this tax in what seemed to be a very unusual way. In order to gain the money needed to pay the tax, Jesus would send Peter fishing. Peter was a skilled fisherman by trade, so Jesus wasn't sending him to do something he had never done before. Jesus was sending him out to use the skills God had given him. It is certain that this fishing trip would be uniquely different than any Peter had been on before, but the act of catching a fish was something he had done countless times before.

God had given Peter a skill set that He would now use to provide for his financial need. Peter's act of fishing was anointed by God to prosper him financially. The work of Peter's hands would yield a monetary reward because the Lord had blessed his labors. This anointing on Peter's work came through the word spoken to him by Jesus. After Peter had a word from Jesus, he moved in faith, and true faith always receives!

God gives certain skill sets to certain people, by which He may use to prosper them. Now, make no mistake, God can prosper and bless His children by any means He wants. Yet, often times He does this through anointing their hands to do certain crafts or skills. The followers of Christ must recognize God's infinite ways of bringing the blessing to them. Like Peter, they must be willing to use the skills God has given them, under the guidance of the Holy Spirit, to gain wealth, so that they may be adequately supplied financially to do the work of the Kingdom.

Moses assured the children of Israel that if they would keep the Lord's commands, He would bless everything they put their hands to. *"The Lord will send a blessing on your barns and on everything you put your hand to. The Lord your God will bless you in the land he is giving you"* (Deuteronomy 28:8, NIV). Israel operated under the Law, but we are under grace, and again, we receive the blessing based off of our relationship with Jesus, and not our works. With this in mind, we should look for the Lord to bless everything we put our hands to!

By the faith that has been given to us in Jesus Christ, we should expectantly look for God to bless and prosper the things we set our hands to. And, we should look for this to happen because of Jesus, and not merely our labors. Faith moves the follower of Christ to put all their strength into the task at hand, and humbly look to God's grace alone to prosper that task! Remember, *"Unless the Lord builds a house, the work of the builders is wasted. Unless the Lord protects a city, guarding it with sentries will do no good. It is useless for you to work so hard from early*

morning until late at night, anxiously working for food to eat;
for God gives rest to his loved ones" (Psalm 127:1-2, NLT).

God Ideas

"Do not say to yourself, 'My power and the might of my own
hand have gotten me this wealth.' But remember the Lord your
God, for it is he who gives you power to get wealth..."
Deuteronomy 8:17-18 (NRSV)

As God brought the children of Israel into the land He had promised to their ancestors, He would give them houses filled with all kinds of good things they did not provide for themselves, wells they did not dig, and vineyards and olive groves they had not planted. On top of all of this, the Lord would also give them the ability to gain financial wealth. This means that God would give them His power to gain wealth in the land they would be living in.

God wanted them to have a firm understanding that even though they may be putting their hand to a certain venture and laboring over that venture, that it was His blessing that was enabling them to be successful at what they were doing and to financially prosper from it. God would give them supernatural ideas, and then He would ensure that as they acted on those ideas which He gave them that they would prosper.

God ideas have the power to bring the wealth of the Kingdom to the children of the King! The power for the children of God to gain wealth lies with their Heavenly Father, who freely gives that power to all who are willing to receive it.

The power to gain wealth implies that often times God expects His children to move in a diligent manner upon the ideas that He speaks to their hearts. Certainly, God is more than able to simply deliver great wealth into the hands of His children by any means He chooses, but, the children of the Kingdom must be open to the leading of their King in the specific business and entrepreneurial ventures they take to gain the wealth God wants to give them. The grace of God, that freely brings financial wealth and prosperity, never makes a person lazy or indifferent, but rather, it makes the follower of Christ industrious and diligent.

Wisdom

The followers of Christ, who show themselves to be both diligent and industrious, are sure to be found moving in the wisdom of God. The Book of Proverbs proclaims that wisdom is more valuable than gold or jewels...how so? For if you give riches such as these to a person who has none, once they use them up, they're back in the same place they once were; broke, destitute, and looking for a handout. But, give a follower of Christ the wisdom needed to gain and maintain wealth, and they will have the power to live free of financial worries and concerns. In speaking of wisdom, the Scriptures declare:

> I, wisdom, live with prudence, and I attain knowledge and discretion. The fear of the Lord is hatred of evil. Pride and arrogance and the way of evil and perverted speech I hate. I have good advice and sound wisdom; I have insight, I have strength. By me kings reign, and rulers decree what is just; by me rulers rule, and nobles, all who govern rightly. I love those who love me, and those who seek me diligently find me. Riches and honor are with me, enduring wealth and prosperity. My fruit is better than gold, even fine gold, and my yield than

choice silver. I walk in the way of righteousness, along the paths of justice, endowing with wealth those who love me, and filling their treasuries (Proverbs 18:12-21, NRSV).

Wisdom brings earthly riches to the followers of Christ who welcomes it in! Wisdom is void of pride, for it realizes that the power it has to gain wealth has come from the Lord. Therefore, the follower of Christ has no room to boast; their wealth has come by the grace of their God. The Apostle Paul, in speaking of how he had diligently labored for the Kingdom of God, said, *"But by the grace of God I am what I am, and his grace toward me has not been in vain. On the contrary, I worked harder than any of them—though it was not I, but the grace of God that is with me"* (1 Corinthians 15:10, NRSV). God's grace had greatly advanced the apostle in his labors, and, even though he had labored diligently, Paul was under no false assumption that it was his own power or might that had advanced him, he knew with certainty that it was God's grace that had provided the means by which he had been able to successfully labor.

Solomon was the third and last king of a united Israel. The Bible paints an extravagant picture of his wealth, when it declares that each year, he received 25 tons of gold, and all of his cups and eating utensils were made out of pure gold. The Bible tells us that he *"had a fleet of trading ships of Tarshish manned by the sailors sent by Hiram. Once every three years the ships returned, loaded with gold, silver, ivory, apes, and peacocks"* (2 Chronicles 9:21, NLT). The Scripture also say, *"King Solomon became richer and wiser than any other king on earth"* (2 Chronicles 19:22). How did Solomon come by all this wealth?

The Bible speaks of when Solomon first became king, and how the Lord came to visit him in his sleep. The Lord asks Solomon what we would desire to have, Solomon replies that he wants wisdom to enable him to lead. Instead of asking for wealth and riches, he asks the Lord for wisdom. Solomon finds that with wisdom, God also brings the ability to gain great wealth. God tells Solomon, *"Because your greatest desire is to help your people, and you did not ask for wealth, riches, fame, or even the death of your enemies or a long life, but rather you asked for wisdom and knowledge to properly govern my people— I will certainly give you the wisdom and knowledge you requested. But I will also give you wealth, riches, and fame such as no other king has had before you or will ever have in the future"* (1 Chronicles 1:11-12, NLT)! Solomon would receive wisdom from God, becoming the wisest king to ever live, and wealth would follow him in all his doings.

The followers of Christ must be cautious not to under value wisdom, for it is a great resource, which is given to the children of God, so that they may gain wealth in their pursuit to advance their Lord's Kingdom. Again, the Book of Proverbs expresses the importance and need for the Christ follower to gain godly wisdom when it says:

> Joyful is the person who finds wisdom, the one who gains understanding. For wisdom is more profitable than silver, and her wages are better than gold. Wisdom is more precious than rubies; nothing you desire can compare with her. She offers you long life in her right hand, and riches and honor in her left. She will guide you down delightful paths; all her ways are satisfying. Wisdom is a tree of life to those who embrace her; happy are those who hold her tightly (Proverbs 3:13-18, NLT).

125

The power to gain wealth lies with our God, His gift of wisdom to His children gives them the ability to possess the wealth He desires them to have. Yet, for wisdom to lead the follower of Christ in paths of blessings and prosperity, they are going to have to move in faith; meaning, they'll need to take the initiative to act on the word of God's guidance (wisdom) He has given them.

Initiative

"The people curse those who hold back grain, but a blessing is on the head of those who sell it." Proverbs 11:26 (NRSV)

To have grain is one thing, but to have the initiative to sell that grain in order to make a profit and help others is quite another. Having the God given wisdom to gain wealth is worthless, unless that wisdom is applied. As we examine initiative and faith, we find that they are closely related. Initiative could be defined as *the ability to willingly do something, or to take action voluntarily*. When someone moves with initiative it is usually done so within an atmosphere of expectation. Faith, as defined by the Scriptures is *"the assurance of things hoped for, the conviction of things not seen"* (Hebrews 11:1, NRSV). It also says, *"faith by itself, if it has no works, is dead"* (James 2:17).

> "Pray as though everything depended on God. Work as though everything depended on you."
>
> Augustine of Hippo

When a follower of Christ takes the initiative to act on a God given idea, with an expectation that their efforts will

126

be prospered by God, in accordance with His word, they are sure to reap a great blessing for their labors. True faith moves the follower of Christ to take the initiative needed to see the wisdom of God bring wealth to their lives and works. Now, we must be careful not to confuse faith, that creates initiative, with actions, designed to create faith. Faith is not created by our actions, rather, faith that is birthed in our hearts by God's word should move us to action.

The two can look similar, but they are quite different. One leads to the follower of Christ being prospered and blessed by God, the other leads to disappointment and confusion. For works, which are driven by mere positive thinking, in hope of creating faith, lack the power of God that brings about His blessing. True faith hears the word of God and is moved to take initiative in starting a new business or perhaps pursuing a new career path, with an expectation that its generous and gracious God will prosper the work of its hands. God will surely bless the work of our hands, but, if we put our hand to nothing, what is there to bless?

Full Nets

The Gospel of Luke tells of a time when Jesus was out preaching the word of God near the Lake of Gennesaret, and the people who were excited to hear the word were crowding against Him. To make some room between Himself and the people, Jesus steps onto a nearby boat. The boat belonged to Simon Peter, who was busy cleaning his nets after a long night of fishing. Peter and his companions had labored all night fishing, but their efforts were to no avail, they had caught nothing.

When Jesus is finished preaching, He urges Simon to put his boat back into the water, and to let his nets down once more. Simon was surely exhausted after working all night and seems to see this request to be a futile venture. Yet, he yields to the word of the Lord, saying, *"Master, we've worked hard all night and haven't caught anything. But because you say so, I will let down the nets"* (Luke 5:5, NIV). Simon and his companions set back out in their boat, and they let down their nets. Unlike their labors of the night past, this time, their nets fill up with fish, so much so, that they must call for help to pull the nets in. The Bible says, *"When they had done so, they caught such a large number of fish that their nets began to break. So they signaled their partners in the other boat to come and help them, and they came and filled both boats so full that they began to sink"* (Luke 5:6-7, NIV).

Simon Peter had labored all night, and his efforts yielded no success, but, when he responded to the word of God in faith, he is prospered beyond anything he could have imagined. Simon's common sense (as we might call it) had to be telling him, *this is foolish*. He had worked all night, he had to be tired and hungry; surely Simon just wanted to get home to his family. But Simon had received a word from God (a God idea) and he acted in faith according to that word and saw the initiative he had taken blessed by the Lord.

Had Simon failed to take the initiative to willingly act on the word of God, he would have missed out on the blessing God desired to give him. Initiative, which was inspired by faith, moved Simon into a position to be financially prospered by God. Faith responds with action to the word of God, and in doing so, receives the blessing of God!

God given ideas must be followed up with initiative! The followers of Christ must possess the faith needed to take the initiative to follow through with that which the Lord leads them to do. If fear and doubt keep us from taking initiative to act in faith on the word of God, we will surely fail to receive the financial blessings of God. Again, if we don't put our hands to the varying ideas God inspires, our hands will produce no work, and therefore there will be nothing to bless. If you want the work of your hands blessed, then put your hands to the work God leads you to, act on the ideas He gives you, be willing to take a step of faith that defies your natural thought process.

Marketing Oil

During the reign of Joram, king of Israel, there lived a woman in the land that owed a debt she could not pay. The woman's husband died and left her indebted to a certain creditor. Unable to pay the debt, the woman faced the threat of her sons being taken as slaves, so that the creditor may recover the money he was owed. The woman's husband had been a member of the company of prophets, so she looks to the Prophet Elisha for help. The prophets of old represented the Lord and spoke the word of God to the people of the land. The prophet inquires of the woman's possessions and finds all she has is a flask of olive oil. Elisha tells the woman, *"Borrow as many empty jars as you can from your friends and neighbors. Then go into your house with your sons and shut the door behind you. Pour olive oil from your flask into the jars, setting each one aside when it is filled"* (2 Kings 4:3-4, NLT).

The widow woman responds in faith, to the word the prophet of God spoke to her and goes out and borrows several jars. She begins to fill the jars with the olive oil she has, as she continues to fill them, her sons continue to go out and borrow more jars. Finally, they come to the point where there are no more jars to be found. *"Soon every container was full to the brim! 'Bring me another jar,' she said to one of her sons. 'There aren't any more!' he told her. And then the olive oil stopped flowing"* (2 Kings 4:6). When this happens, the widow woman reports to the prophet, looking for further instructions, Elisha tells her *"Now sell the olive oil and pay your debts, and you and your sons can live on what is left over"* (2 Kings 4:7).

The woman starts off with a desperate need and looks to the Prophet Elisha for help. The prophet, representing God upon the earth, spoke the word of God to this woman. The widow woman received the word, but for God's word to profit her she was going to need to move in faith, taking the initiative to put her hands to the task of acquiring jars and filling them with oil. If the woman doesn't take initiative, responding to the word of God in faith, she would have missed the financial blessing of God, which He was trying to give her.

If she did not put her hands to this task, there would have been nothing to bless. God's supernatural provision was seen in the abundance of olive oil produced from a small amount. His favor on this idea can be seen in the ability of the brothers to borrow jars. The full realization of God's provision was made manifest once the final step of faith was taken, and the widow takes the initiative to go out and sell the oil. Had the widow woman failed to take initiative on the God idea she had received, she would have failed to receive the financial blessing God desired to give to her. Initiative made the way for the blessing of God to be fully realized in her life!

Remember, faith brings the blessings of God to full maturity in our lives, and, our works, or lack thereof, are sure to testify of our faith! When the word of God is received and embraced, faith in that word is birthed, and when that happens the follower of Christ is moved to take action, which is sure to bring the full measure of God's blessing upon us. Consider this:

> And it is impossible to please God without faith. Anyone who wants to come to him must believe that God exists and that he rewards those who sincerely seek him. It was by faith that Noah built a large boat to save his family from the flood. He obeyed God, who warned him about things that had never happened before. By his faith Noah condemned the rest of the world, and he received the righteousness that comes by faith (Hebrews 11:6-7, NLT).

Noah received a word from God, which birthed faith in his heart causing him to take action. He put his hands to the task of building an ark, and God blessed the work of his hands. Noah took initiative, and that initiative brought the blessing of God to a full realization in his life!

The widow woman had to go to the Prophet Elisha to receive a word from God, but this was before the death and resurrection of Jesus Christ. Now, every Christ follower has the Holy Spirit living in them; by God's Spirit they can experience God speaking to them directly, either through the Scriptures or directly to their heart. Because of this, we are able to look to God for a word concerning our financial situation; once we receive a word from God, we must embrace that word as absolute truth! When the word of God that has been spoken to us is embraced as truth, faith will surely spring up in our hearts, moving us to take initiative (that is to act on God's word for our lives), and that initiative will usher in the financial blessings of God, so that the followers of Christ will lack nothing as they wage war against the enemy for the souls of mankind!

Unescapable Blessings

Joseph was the second youngest son of Jacob, and his father favored him above all his other brothers. This created a great deal of jealousy in the eyes of his older brothers. One day, while still a young man, Joseph has a dream about how God would lift him up above all his brothers, shortly afterwards, he had a second dream confirming how he would rule over his entire family. Joseph told the dream to his father and brothers, but it only served to fuel the fire of his brother's resentment towards him.

One day, while away from their father, Joseph's brothers plot an evil scheme and sell their brother to slave traders, and then fabricate a lie to make their father believe he was killed by a wild beast. The traders take Joseph to Egypt where they sell him to Potiphar, an officer of Pharaoh, the king of Egypt. At this point Joseph must have thought the dreams God gave him were nothing more than his foolish teenage imagination. But those dreams were from God, and as long as Joseph remained faithful to God, and continued to trust Him, nothing would stop the Lord Almighty from blessing him!

While with Potiphar, the Bible says, *"The Lord was with Joseph, so he succeeded in everything he did as he served in the home of his Egyptian master"* (Genesis 39:2, NLT). Potiphar saw that God was prospering Joseph, so he put everything under Joseph's control, and sure enough, everything Joseph put his hands to God blessed. With Joseph in charge of Potiphar's affairs everything he owned prospered, so much so, that *"with Joseph there, he didn't worry about a thing—except what kind of food to eat"* (Genesis 39:6, NLT)!

Being a slave couldn't stop the blessing of God from abounding in the life of Joseph! For Joseph refused to sit back and feel sorry for himself! Joseph didn't consider the limits of his circumstance, but the limitlessness of His God! Even as a slave, everything Joseph put his hands to prospered!

Joseph's success in Potiphar's house would be brought to an end by Potiphar's lying wife, who wanted to have a sinful affair with Joseph, but, when Joseph refuses to sin against God, she fabricated a story that gets him thrown into prison. At this point who could have blamed Joseph if he just set down in his misery and sulked. It had to seem like he was being punished for doing the right thing; surely, he must have felt confused and frustrated. Yet, Joseph does not allow his circumstances to define his life! He continues to trust in God, and God continues to bless everything he touches. The Bible says, *"The Lord was with Joseph in the prison and showed him his faithful love. And the Lord made Joseph a favorite with the prison warden. Before long, the warden put Joseph in charge of all the other prisoners and over everything that happened in the prison. The warden had no more worries, because Joseph took care of everything. The Lord was with him and caused everything he did to succeed"* (Genesis 39:21-23, NLT).

Again, regardless of where Joseph found himself, the blessing of God was with him, and prospered him in everything he did. Joseph didn't allow circumstance to keep him down, but continued to trust in God, and continued to reap the rewards of faith! Joseph's actions demonstrated the faith that permeated inside his heart, and that faith continually led Joseph to take initiative wherever he found himself.

> "God never withholds from His child that which His love and wisdom call good. God's refusals are always merciful- 'severe mercies' at times but mercies all the same. God never denies us our hearts desire except to give us something better."
>
> Elisabeth Eliot

God's blessing on His children cannot be hindered by circumstance, only by a lack of faith! As both a slave and a prisoner, Joseph experienced the blessing of God prospering him in everything he put his hands to. Had Joseph failed to put his hands to anything, and chose to sulk in his misery, making excuses for why God wasn't blessing him and why he couldn't be successful, he would've missed the grace and kindness of his loving God! The Scriptures warn us about making excuses, saying, *"The lazy person claims, 'There's a lion out there! If I go outside, I might be killed'"* (Proverbs 22:13, NLT)! Refuse to make excuses about why you can't be successful, and fix in your heart the belief that God is with you, and regardless of your situation, you will be successful, you will be prospered, and everything you put your hand to will be blessed by your gracious God!

Joseph would eventually find himself in Pharaoh's palace as a prince over Egypt, but the path to the promise of God was not quick or easy, but it was blessed by God, and, it was fully realized through Joseph's willingness to take the initiative to put his hands to work regardless of his situation. Initiative requires faith, and faith always receives the blessings of God! Whether that faith is found in slavery, in a prison, or in a palace, it is always honored by God, who uses it as a doorway to send His blessing and favor through to His children! If you want the abounding blessings of God to continually overflow in your life, never close the door of faith!

Humble Beginnings

David Green is the billionaire that founded Hobby Lobby. If you're not familiar with Hobby Lobby, it's a chain of stores that specialize in selling arts and crafts supplies. Green started the company in 1972, with only $600, today there are about 600 Hobby Lobby stores throughout the U.S. Green founded the business on biblical principles, and still runs it that way today. Green had a knack for the retail business, and when he put his hand to it, God blessed him. Green's gifting was in the retail business, it was something God blessed him to do. Doing what God called him to do, he found himself abundantly blessed.

Green's walk of faith is surely demonstrated in his actions; he and his family have given millions of dollars to Christian causes and education, and still today the retail giant continues to do business according to biblical principles. The organization has chaplains within its stores, and regularly shares the Gospel message with its employees. In an interview with CBN, Green said, "*I would like to know that we have brought as many people to know Christ as we possibly can.*" He went on to say, "*We hope to continue to just grow our company. As long as there's someone on this earth that doesn't know Jesus Christ, we have a job to do.*"[2] David Green obviously saw his purpose wasn't just to make money, but to make disciples and further the Kingdom of his God.

If God has anointed you in a certain way, don't be afraid to pursue that anointing, so that God may financially prosper you through it! Small beginnings can end up experiencing large rewards; especially when the child of God moves in faith, taking initiative as the Spirit leads them! But, always remember, your purpose is not to make money and gain wealth. Wealth and money are simply tools; tools to be used by the children of God to advance His Kingdom, as they pursue the fulfillment of the Great Commission their King has given to all His followers!

[2] Green, David (December, 2017) Retrieved from:
http://www1.cbn.com/content/david-green-biblical-principles-business

Application and Self-Reflection

1. How would you describe faith?

_____

_____

_____

2. What role has initiative, or a lack thereof, played in your current financial situation?

_____

_____

_____

3. How have you experienced the correlation that exists between faith and initiative?

_____

_____

_____

4. Have you received a God given idea? If so, what is it?

_____

_____

_____

5. What are at least 3 steps you could immediately take to see this idea become a reality?

_____

_____

_____

6. What could hinder you from taking these initial steps?

_____

_____

_____

7. How could this hindrance be overcome?

_____

_____

_____

Chapter 8

A Poverty Mind

"The blessing of the Lord makes a person rich, and he adds no sorrow with it." Proverbs 10:22 (NLT)

Several years ago, we had a visiting missionary who was going to be in the area stop by the church to share the Word with us. Ron and Christi had been friends of the church for many years (long before I was the pastor), so most of the congregation at the time were familiar with them. Since I've been the pastor, we've always given generously to missionaries to help them on a monthly basis, as well as giving generous honorariums to those who come to the church to speak.

Ron spoke that Sunday as planned, and afterwards we had lunch and enjoyed a time of fellowship. We had prepared a generous offering to give to Ron and Christi, but the Lord spoke to my heart at lunch to increase the amount we were giving, which would have nearly doubled what we had previously decided on. The amount we had predetermined was already going to stretch the church, but to nearly double that amount seemed ridiculous.

I dismissed the Lord's prompting as my own thoughts, but that was only because the amount of money He wanted us to give away was beyond my natural understanding. After we finished lunch, we gave them their offering and said goodbye. I felt satisfied that the honorarium we gave them was a good one, and in truth, by all-natural accounts it was.

It was Sunday about two in the afternoon that we saw Ron and Christi off. The next morning around 8am I was in the sanctuary of the church praying, when I was startled by a lady tapping me on the shoulder. She and her family attended church about once every other month, so I was surprised to see her at the church during a Monday morning prayer service. She had a check in her hand and said her and her husband wanted to give a tithe to the church. I took the check and looked at the amount it was made out for…can you guess how much it was for? The exact difference between what we had given Ron and Christi and what the Lord told us to give. I immediately had that amount sent to them!

Less than 24 hours after God had told me to give an amount that I felt was beyond our ability (and lacked the faith to simply trust Him to provide) He graciously brought the money that He wanted us to give. The money He wanted me to trust Him for! But, a poverty mindset (which I would have never associated myself with) hindered my ability to move in faith; simply trusting God to provide and depending on the abundance of His storeroom.

A poverty mindset is not determined by your physical assets, it's determined by our inability to trust God for our full provision. A poverty mindset doesn't walk by faith, but gages what it can and cannot do only by the amount of money and assets that it has in hand. A poverty mindset is limited by its natural circumstances, and therefore is restricted from moving in faith and experiencing the fullness of God's financial provision.

As we embrace the truth of God's word, which says, *"The blessing of the Lord makes a person rich, and he adds no sorrow with it"* (Proverbs 10:22, NRSV). Our minds will be free from the curse of poverty, that the enemy uses to restrain and constrict our ability to freely receive financial provision from the Lord, so that we may advance the Mission of our Lord. Believe God's word...Act on God's word...and, the riches of His financial blessings will be at your disposal, as you labor to advance the Kingdom of your God!

The Psychology of Poverty

"For as he thinks in his heart, so is he." Proverbs 23:7 (NKJ)

The word *"think"* used here is the Hebrew word *"sha`ar"* meaning *"to act as gate-keeper"*. So, our thoughts can literally act as a gatekeeper, who opens us up to receive the blessing, promises, and power of God, or, who closes us off from receiving them all! How we perceive wealth and poverty, and the role and use of money in our lives, will often dictate whether or not our financial state is one of scarcity or abundance. The way we think about money, and, our right and ability to have it, affects the reality of our financial position.

The poverty mindset acts from a perception of scarcity; it sees itself in a constant state of lack, and therefore has great difficulty receiving the abundance that God has made available to His children. Research has shown that scarcity effects the way we make decisions, it determines how we see and perceive reality.[3] God's children who are trapped in poverty act from a mindset of scarcity, which keeps them trapped in a continual loop of financial lack.

When God's children (or anyone) are living with the mentality of scarcity it influences their cognitive ability.[4] They are less

---

[3] Shah, Anuj K., Eldar Shafir, and Sendhil Mullainathan. "Scarcity Frames Value." Psychological Science (0956-7976) 26, no. 4 (2015): 402-12.
[4] Mani, Anandi, Sendhil Mullainathan, Eldar Shafir, and Jiaying Zhao. "Poverty Impedes Cognitive Function." Science (New York, N.Y.) 341, no. 6149 (2013):

likely to accurately apply God's word to their lives and circumstances. They move in a fearful state of not having enough, feeling that every act that involves their financial resources (which they currently perceive as their own) will involve some form of trade-off.[5] God's children who have a poverty mindset, operate in the ministry God has called them to with the idea that they will not have enough money to do that ministry and to provide for their personal needs. They focus on their pressing needs for food, shelter, and clothing, discounting the promise of their Lord to provide all those things for them as they actively seek His Kingdom. Their cognitive ability to grasp the promise of God to provide for all their needs is hindered by the scarcity/poverty they live in, which always involves the idea of a tradeoff, which will result in some form of loss if they follow through with what the Lord has called them to do. They live in a state of wanting to do for the Lord but limited by their ability to embrace His promised provision.

The poverty that many individuals of the world are faced with can largely be contributed to a negative emotional state.[6] They are faced with the mentality that they are not good enough, or do not possess the ability to escape the cycle of poverty, which they have been faced with for so much of their lives. A majority of people who live in poverty will find it is a generational condition that their parents, and perhaps even their grandparents, have not been able to break free from.

976-80.

[5] Shah, Anuj K., Eldar Shafir, and Sendhil Mullainathan. "Scarcity Frames Value." Psychological Science (0956-7976) 26, no. 4 (2015): 402-12.

[6] Johan Janse van, Rensburg. "The Psychology of Poverty." Verbum et Ecclesia 34, no. 1 (2013): 1.

Those who live trapped in a state of poverty with a mindset framed by scarcity often find themselves plagued with thoughts of unworthiness, thoughts that lead them to a false belief that they're poor because *they're no good*, or simply *not good enough*.[7] These lies from the enemy create a feeling of inferiority in the children of God, and over a period of time God's children who are trapped in poverty begin to believe the devil's lies.

The children of God who are stuck in poverty are no less able to make money and experience the abundance of their Father's storehouse than anyone else! They are merely distracted by the lies of the enemy and the reality of their circumstance. They know what the Scriptures proclaim about God's provision and His willingness to give His people the power to gain wealth, but their cognitive ability to grasp the Scriptures as practical truth is diluted by their poverty mindset. Individuals trapped by a poverty mindset often find themselves making the wrong or unproductive decisions concerning their finances time and again.[8]

Perception

"One person gives freely, yet gains even more; another withholds unduly, but comes to poverty." Proverbs 11:24 (NIV)

It makes little sense to the natural mind that as we give freely of the finances God has entrusted us with that we will gain even more, and if we cling to those finances, unwilling to let them freely go, we will surely experience poverty. Shouldn't it be the

---

[7] ibid

[8] Mani, Anandi, Sendhil Mullainathan, Eldar Shafir, and Jiaying Zhao. "Poverty Impedes Cognitive Function." Science (New York, N.Y.) 341, no. 6149 (2013): 976-80.

opposite? Shouldn't it be: the more we keep back for ourselves, the more we save, and the more we store-up, the more we have? And, doesn't it make sense, that the more we give away, the less we'll have? The things that make sense to our natural mind, especially when it comes to wealth and money, seldom coincide with the Word of God. God's Word declares that as we freely give in faith of the finances we have, for the furtherance of His Kingdom, those finances will be returned to us in an increased amount.

Freely giving in faith causes us to freely receive even more, because at that point faith is involved, and, it is by faith that we receive from the Lord! Yet, holding on to the money we have, because of a poverty mindset that is motivated by the concept of scarcity, causes the child of God to remain in a state of poverty. The child of God wrongly perceives as truth that they must cling to the little they have if they want their basic needs to be met. They feel there will be a tradeoff of some kind if they give to help those in need or to further the Kingdom of God. They look for, and truly feel it is the responsibility of others who have more, to give towards the work of the Kingdom. Now it is true, that the more we have been given the more responsibility we have towards the work of the Kingdom. But it is also a Kingdom truth, that if the children of God wrongly contribute the reasons for poverty and wealth to worldly principles, they will reap according to the principles of the world and not according to the principles of their God. *"Don't be misled: No one makes a fool of God. What a person plants, he will harvest. The person who plants selfishness, ignoring the needs of others—ignoring God!—harvests a crop of weeds. All he'll have to show for his life is weeds! But the one who plants in response to God, letting*

God's Spirit do the growth work in him, harvests a crop of real life, eternal life" (Galatians 6:7-8, MSG).

The perceptual process is the process by which each individual determines in their minds and hearts what is real and what is not. The perceptual process could be defined as, the cognitive process by which an individual selects, organizes, and gives meaning to environmental stimuli.[9] Perception, whether right or wrong, is how we each determine reality. Yes, as a child of God we should base every truth we hold off of the Scriptures. But even though we will declare the Scriptures, which speak about God's generosity and provision towards His children, as absolute truths, we often behave contrary to these truths when it comes to our finances. For most individuals, perception is their primary source of knowledge, and as such they seldom bring that perceived knowledge into question.[10] Now, it is possible for this perception to be formed from flawed information, or moments of disappointment and confusion that we may have encountered surrounding our finances. These moments can cause us to form a miss-perception about the way God works when it comes to money and wealth. Even though this perception that was formed contradicts the Scriptures, because we faithfully embrace it in our actions and behavior, it becomes a self-imposed reality that keeps us from experiencing the generosity of our Father, as it pertains to our finances.

The Bible reminds us of a time when Jesus was forced to confront a miss-perception that was held by the people of His day. This miss-perception guided their actions and behaviors,

---

[9] Konopaske, R., Ivancevich, J., & Matteson, M. (2018). Organizational Behavior & Management (11 ed.). New York: McGraw Hill.
[10] Moustakas, C. E. (1994). Phenomenological research methods. Thousand Oaks, Calif: Sage.

but once Jesus confronts it and corrects it, the door is opened for God's provision (which would come in the form of healing) to be received. In studying this scenario, which is found in John chapter nine, we can learn how to correct our own miss-perceptions, so that we may be free to receive from the bountiful goodness of God's provision. The story reads:

> As he went along, he saw a man blind from birth. His disciples asked him, "Rabbi, who sinned, this man or his parents, that he was born blind?" "Neither this man nor his parents sinned," said Jesus, "but this happened so that the works of God might be displayed in him. As long as it is day, we must do the works of him who sent me. Night is coming, when no one can work. While I am in the world, I am the light of the world." After saying this, he spit on the ground, made some mud with the saliva, and put it on the man's eyes. "Go," he told him, "wash in the Pool of Siloam" (this word means "Sent"). So the man went and washed, and came home seeing (John 9:1-7. NIV)

There are two steps we can see Jesus taking as He confronts this miss-perception: He identifies the miss-perception and corrects it. He then creates a new perception based on the reality of Scripture. Let's first look at the miss-perception that was held by most individuals within the culture.

As Jesus and the disciples come up on this blind man the question of sin arises. In the eyes of the disciples and other Jews of the day, handicaps such as blindness were brought on by sin. Suffering, sickness, and deformities were seen as consequences of sin. In the sight of the disciples this blind man was afflicted with blindness due to sin. The only question in the minds of the disciples was whose sin caused his affliction. Based on the perception (which was false) held by the disciples, someone had to have sinned for this affliction to be on this man. The cultural perception of sin and suffering dictated how the disciples saw this man, and if not for Jesus, would also dictate their behavior towards him and their willingness, or lack thereof, to help him.

Perceptual errors occur when individuals misinterpret the countless circumstances they are confronted with. What does this mean for the child of God? It means that when their perception is incorrect, the actions they take based on that perception will not produce the outcome they desire. So, when God's children attempt to increase their financial position based on worldly wisdom, discounting the absolute and infallible truth of God's Word, they are faced with continued financial lack and frustration. As it concerns worldly wisdom, and the perspectives we build around worldly concepts, the Bible warns us by saying, *"There is a way that seems right to a person, but its end is the way to death"* (Proverbs 14:12, NRSV).

Part of the perceptual process that leads to decision making is focus. Individuals select which occurrences in their environment they will focus on, this focus can be good, but, if it is not on the truth of God's word it can limit their ability to trust God, walking in faithful obedience to His Word. When this happens, it creates a phenomenon that can be referred to as bounded awareness.[11] Bounded awareness causes God's children to ignore certain truths concerning His Word that are needed to make good decisions regarding their actions, and

---

[11] Bazerman, M., & Chugh, D. (2006, January). Decisions Without Blinders. Harvard Business Review.

motives, when it comes to money. This often occurs because they are focused on some particular frustration or disappointment they have experienced in the past. God's children must possess the ability to expand the limits of their awareness, so that they may make financial decisions in a Scriptural manner, led by the Holy Spirit, based on the entire Word of God, and not just the information that is perceived from a bounded focus.

Researchers have found that the same part of the brain used to make decisions based on commonly held knowledge (which would be knowledge gained by reading it directly from the Bible) is also used to make decision based off of perceived-truths that have been formed within our mind, based solely off of our experiences (even if those perceived-truths, which have been formed off of our experiences contradict Scriptural knowledge).[12] For the follower of Christ this means that even when we have the truths of the Scripture, previously formed perception, based off of past experiences, can cause us to make decisions that are in direct contradiction to what the Bible says is true, because our focus is still on the negative experience that created the false perception we cling to. Miss-perception must be corrected if the followers of Christ are going to live in the financial provision their Father in Heaven is willing to give them.

Now, what steps did Jesus take to correct the perception of His followers in John chapter nine?

---

[12] Kovács, Á. M., Kühn, S., Gergely, G., Csibra, G., & Brass, M. (2014). Are All Beliefs Equal? Implicit Belief Attributions Recruiting Core Brain Regions of Theory of Mind.

1) He identified the miss-perception and provided the correct focus.

Jesus, as the disciple's teacher, corrects their miss-perception when He tells them that the man was not suffering from blindness as a consequence of sin. The disciples observed the man was blind, it was at this point they chose to focus on sin, and the consequences thereof, but their selected focus is redirected by Jesus. Jesus is not focused on sin, but on the glory of God. Jesus turns the attention of the disciples to the possibility of God being glorified from this sickness, which was a thought that contradicted the cultural attitude towards sickness and sin at the time. Jesus corrects the disciple's perception, which was created by the cultural dynamics of the time, so that they could correctly focus on the many suffering individuals of their world that they were certain to encounter, as they went about their mission to make disciples of all nations.

When Jesus corrects what the disciples believe to be true about the cause for the blindman's affliction, He immediately brings them to a new focus, which was the glory of God. As followers of Christ, we must identify our miss-perceptions that do not line up with the truth of God's Word, particularly concerning wealth and finances. We must refocus our attention to the realities declared in God's Word and not the destructive works and lies the enemy has tricked us into embracing. When we do change our focus, the way we understand our circumstances and our environment will change, causing us to respond to the Word of God with the right perspective, which in-turn, will bring about the desired outcome concerning our financial position. We must objectively challenge the beliefs that we hold to be true that directly contradict the word of God and hinder us from acting in faith, so that the all the blessings of God may overflow our lives, which most certainly includes financial blessings!

Scientific research has proven this to be true. Researchers, in studying the power of perception to dictate our action and behavior, found that sensory processing produced an image that was an accurate reproduction to the physical stimuli that individuals were subjected to, regardless of the eventual decision they would make.[13] They also found that the sensory representation remained stable when a decision had to be made that related to that stimuli, but if the task at hand was unrelated the sensory representation varied with time. What does this research mean for the follower of Christ? It means that the way we process the varying experiences we are subject to, and the decisions we make based on those experiences, will remain unchanged, unless the way in which we have selected to view those experiences is changed and redirected. The perception of the Christ follower can be changed, and indeed must be, if it is faulty, causing them to act in fear and doubt, outside the faith Jesus has given them, so that they may not be hindered by financial lack in their efforts to expand the Kingdom of God.

2) He Prompted an Act of Faith.

After Jesus makes mud with His saliva and dirt, placing it on the eyes of the blind man, He instructs Him to go in the pool of Siloam. John reminds his reader that the word Siloam means sent, denoting an attitude of obedience that the blind man would need to receive his eyesight back. The blind man's focus is not the mud made from spit, or the suffering he has endured as a blind beggar, but on the words of Jesus to go and wash in the

---

[13] Mostert, P., Kok, P., & Lange, F. P. d. (2015). Dissociating sensory from decision processes in human perceptual decision making.

pool of Siloam. The perspective of any true disciple of Jesus must bring them to a place of obedience, where they attribute their decision making to the trust they have placed in Jesus.

The pool of Siloam was fed by the stream Siloah (or Shiloah) which was associated with the promise of the Messiah in the Old Testament. The Prophet Isaiah wrote, *"Because this people has refused the waters of Shiloah that flow gently, and melt in fear before Rezin and the son of Remaliah"* (Isaiah 8:6). John points to the fact that the promised Messiah has come, which he does throughout his account of the Gospel. Both the healing of the blind man and the details surrounding the healing point to the fact that Jesus is the Messiah. With an honest perspective that Jesus is the Messiah, the current disciples and future disciples of Jesus will respond to Him in obedience, as the blind man did, because their focus is on the Messiah and not the suffering and trials, which all followers of Christ will surely face.

The method Jesus uses to bring about a knew perception in the blind man and the disciples leads us to the conclusion that action will be required to create a new and lasting perception (scientific research on perception reveals the same truth). As the focus of individual followers of Christ is shifted on the way they view wealth and money, a corresponding action will need to be taken to validate the new perspective for it truly to take root. The miss-perception that first century Jewish people had on the correlation between sin and suffering would be broken both in the minds of the disciples, and the blindman, only when the blind man took action on the words of Jesus, and a new perception was established in their minds.

What we think in the depths of our being will always be displayed in our actions. Even though the follower of Christ may have a head knowledge of what God's Word declares about wealth and money, they must also develop a heart knowledge, which means they must hold the right perception about wealth. For whatever is in the heart of a believer will eventually be displayed in the reality of their life. Miss-perceptions about wealth will result in poverty and lack. When the follower of Christ has the right perspective on the blessings of God, the devil can resist them all he wants, but sooner or later the riches of God's provision will be made manifest in their lives, and they will be fully supplied financially to do all the Lord places within their hearts.

Destined to be Blessed

"Real help comes from God. Your blessing clothes your people!" Psalm 3:8 (MSG)

The follower of Christ is clothed in the blessing of God, because of the work of Jesus! Our financial help and provision are sure to come from only one source, and that source is our God. If we look to anyone else, or any other source, for our financial provision we will miss the blessing of God! Yes, we may find a source of revenue and provision, but it will pale in comparison to what we could have through Jesus Christ; given to us by the hand of our Father. To live in this manner, we must have the

> "It is the heart that makes a man rich. He is rich or poor according to what he is, not according to what he has."
>
> Henry Beecher

right perception of ourselves and our God. If our perception on either is corrupted by the world we live in, we'll never have the financially blessed life we were destined to have. Even as we labor to expand the Kingdom of our Lord, if the way we view our relationship with God and money is wrong, we will labor in financial frustration; as many followers of Christ do.

History records the inspiring life of a woman named Bridget "Biddy" Mason. Biddy was born into slavery and remained a slave for a large part of her life. But God had plans for Biddy that no slave owner could stop. God strategically placed people in Biddy's path who encouraged her to petition for her freedom while in the state of California. Biddy takes their advice, and not only petitions the state for her freedom, but for the freedom of 19 others, and, by the grace of God wins her case. Biddy obviously saw herself as more than a slave with the potential to do great things. Her perspective of her life and her God were not defined by her circumstances, which were surely grievous and oppressive.

Once freed, Biddy would eventually become a successful black businesswoman, which living in the 1800's was no small feat. She worked as a midwife for 10 years, being payed $2.50 a day, and helping those who could not afford her services by doing the work for free. Eventually she saved enough money to purchase some land, becoming one of the first black women to own land in the United States. She then sold off some of the land for a profit and built a commercial building on the other property; renting out storefronts and living in the upstairs section with her family. Biddy used the wisdom God gave her to move forward into the financial blessings of God.

Biddy amassed a small financial fortune through her shrewd business practices. She was known throughout the community as "Grandma Mason", for she graciously helped the poor and needy in the community, and, regularly went to visit inmates in the local prison. Biddy financed the first black church building in the community; she used the financial resources God had blessed her with to further the advancement of her Lord's Kingdom. Her great-granddaughter Gladys Owens Smith quoted her as saying, *"If you hold your hand closed, nothing good can come in. The open hand is blessed, for it gives in abundance, even as it receives."*

Despite growing up a slave with every reason to hold a negative image of herself, the world around her, and even God, Biddy made a choice to look beyond her present circumstance, and embrace the possibilities that were available to her through the grace of a supernatural God; who made the impossible into the possible for His children! She didn't perceive herself through a poverty mindset. Even though she grew up in poverty and slavery, she refused to embrace that mentality.

We must allow the Scriptures to frame our perspective on life and money. Understanding that God's ways will seldom make sense to the natural mind, and it is from the natural mind that the poverty mindset is birthed. Take for instance Proverbs 11:24, which says, *""One person gives freely, yet gains even more; another withholds unduly, but comes to poverty"* (NIV). The natural way of doing things says, *"a penny saved is a penny earned."* A poverty mindset fears not having enough, and therefore hold tightly to that which it has. Yet, the Scriptures declare it is possible to save and hold on to your money, and at the same time suffer want. God's way of doing things says, *"give freely in faith, that flows from a love of God, and you will grow richer.*" With God, we find an inverse relationship between cause and effect, which opposes our natural way of thinking. Holding back money will lead a person to suffer want, while freely giving (which should be done in faith that flows from a love of God) causes a person to grow richer. Yield your mind to the truth of the Scriptures, and you will see the abundance of God's riches overflow your life!

Application and Self-Reflection

1. How might a poverty mentality be affecting you?

_____

_____

_____

2. How do you perceive giving your finances to the work of the Kingdom?

_____

_____

_____

3. How does a lack of money hinder you?

_____

_____

_____

4. How could this hindrance be overcome?

_____

_____

_____

5. List at least three perspectives you hold on money and wealth, and then match those perspectives up with examples of biblical characters who also held them and tell how those perceptions effected their lives.

_____
_____
_____
_____
_____
_____
_____

6. Tell of a time when you encountered financial disappointment, and how that disappointment hindered your labors for Christ.

_____
_____
_____

7. Does that disappointment still hinder you today? If so, what are some steps you could take to overcome it?

_____
_____
_____

Summary

"Everyone then who hears these words of mine and acts on them will be like a wise man who built his house on rock."
Matthew 7:24 (NRSV)

The blessings of the Kingdom are for the children of the King, so that they may advance the Kingdom of their God free of financial frustrations and limitations!

I encourage you to take the biblical principles that have been presented in this book and apply them to your life. If they are not applied, even if you recognize them as Scriptural truths, they will in no way benefit you.

<u>**Remember**</u>:

1) Stay humble at all times and in all things! Humility will open the door to more of the blessings of God (including the financial ones) than you could ever imagine!

2) Fix in your heart that it's ok for you (as a follower of Christ) to be blessed with money! For that money is a tool for you to use in your pursuit to advance the Kingdom of your God.

3) Remember the blessing can come to you in a variety of ways, so don't limit God to some rigid format that you've created in your mind. Be open to the Lord blessing you however He chooses! Don't reject God's

blessings and gifts just because they don't come packaged the way you expected them to!

4) The blessings of God will come to you only by faith! They are based off the works of Jesus and not your own. So, move in faith according to the Word of God; for faith without works is nothing more than a fading mirage.

5) God is your loving Father, and He is with you always! Stay aware of the abiding presence of your Heavenly Father, and the blessings that come from being in His presence.

6) What you think about money and the blessings of God matter! You are a child of the King, and your Father owns the abundance of this world, so think blessed!

7) God will bless the work of your hands, so be sure to take the initiative to put your hands to work! If you refuse to put your hands to something, there will be nothing for God to bless!

8) Understand that a poverty mindset will keep you from experiencing the financial blessings of God. Therefore, those behavior patterns concerning money that do not line up with the Word of God must be changed! Identify what your incorrect perceptions are, and then change your focus and purposely act on what the Scriptures proclaim.

Made in the USA
Columbia, SC
21 October 2024

44556151R00098